Quick & Easy
Hot and Spicy

p

Contents

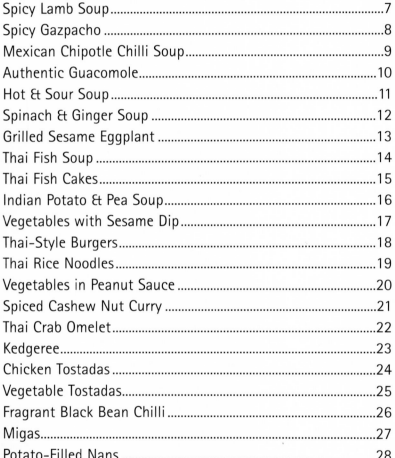

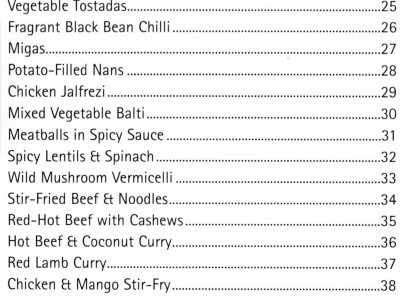

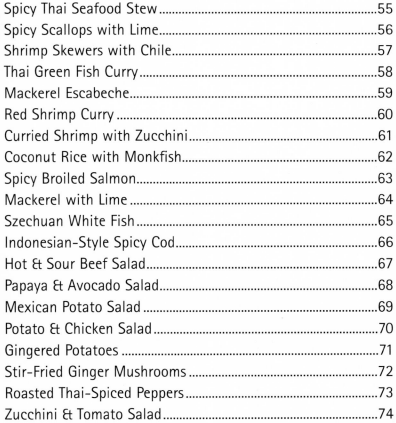

Introduction

Changing tastes and a more daring approach to what we eat have led in recent years to a growing interest in food from many different cultures. Among the most popular cuisines are those from China, India, Thailand, Mexico—anywhere, in fact, that serves hot and spicy dishes, bursting with new and exciting flavors that sometimes make your eyes water, as well as your mouth. Soups, fish, meat, chicken, and vegetables are transformed with the addition of chiles, ginger, and garlic, and with a range of dried spices. The recipes in this book are quick and easy to make, but still impressive: you can create something really special for a special occasion, and you can even top it off with a hot and spicy dessert.

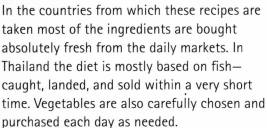

Pantry items

In the countries from which these recipes are taken most of the ingredients are bought absolutely fresh from the daily markets. In Thailand the diet is mostly based on fish—caught, landed, and sold within a very short time. Vegetables are also carefully chosen and purchased each day as needed.

However, there are some items that can be kept at hand. Rice is the most important staple food, either forming the basis of the main dish or, more often, served as a side dish, perhaps with herbs, spices, or vegetables added. Long-grain white rice and Indian basmati rice with its distinctive aroma and flavor are staples and readily available in large stores. They will keep for quite a while in an airtight container. Noodles are another staple, used frequently in Chinese and Thai cooking where they are tossed in a wok with meat or fish and vegetables, and seasoned generously. They come in many forms and among the most popular are rice noodles, almost transparent and shaped as flat ribbons or thin vermicelli, and the egg noodles favored by the Chinese, a rich yellow in color and crinkled in shape. Both types are not so much cooked as softened by soaking in boiling water for just a few minutes.

A range of oils is also useful, and some of these will already be kept in the pantry for general use. Sunflower oil and vegetable oil are the most widely used, because they are light and mild, complementing the food rather than flavoring it. Olive oil is

commonly used in some cuisines, notably Mexican, and it is best to choose a really good virgin olive oil. It is also worth investing in a bottle of sesame oil made from roasted sesame seeds and full of flavor. This is not used for cooking food because it burns easily. Instead, it is drizzled over the finished dish. And for the very brave, a bottle of chili oil is hot stuff indeed.

Beans are often used as the basis of spicy dishes because they readily absorb the delicious flavors of the food. The classic is the ever-popular Mexican chili-bean stew, warming and filling. When using beans you have two options: you can buy packets of dried beans, which are very cheap and keep well, but have to be soaked overnight before cooking; or you can buy cans of ready-cooked beans which are a little more expensive but very useful if you want to rustle up a quick dish for lunch or for an evening dish midweek.

Also readily available, and ideal for anyone with limited spare time are the jars of sauces and pastes stocked by food stores everywhere. Using bottled sauces is not quite the same as making them from scratch, but they still taste good. Green and red Thai curry pastes can be used for a fast green fish curry or a red lamb curry. Indian curry pastes range from mild to extremely hot. Many of the recipes in this book need dried spices, such as cumin, coriander, cardamom, and turmeric. Their

flavor deteriorates rapidly, so, unless you are planning to do a lot of this type of cooking, buy them in small quantities and store them in a cool, dark place. Also add some authentic seasoning sauces to your pantry—soy sauce, which is made from fermented soy beans, and Thai fish sauce, made from salted fermented fish.

Chiles, Ginger, and Garlic

All these items add a real zing to your hot and spicy, cooking, but it is fair to say that when it comes to heat, chiles are the star. There are many varieties of chile, and different cultures favor different ones, so it is worth looking out for the right one for a particular dish. Many recipes call for chiles, but dried crushed chilis may be substituted. Some chiles are quite mild, while others are fiery hot—larger chiles are usually milder than small ones, and red chiles tend to be a little sweeter and milder than green ones. If you are in any doubt about eating a dish seasoned with chiles, bear in mind that most of the heat is in the seeds, so, if you remove these before cooking, the dish will not be so fiery.

Thai dishes often include bird-eye chiles. These are small and either red or green, and they are very, very hot. In Mexico, where chiles of one variety or another are included in virtually every recipe, the small green variety called jalapeño is especially popular, and dried chilis—ancho and chipotle—are also used.

Chiles are extremely irritating to the skin, so if you are particularly sensitive, wear rubber gloves when preparing them, and if you are removing the seeds, do so with the point of a sharp knife. Always wash your hands really thoroughly afterward, and make sure you keep your hands away from your eyes.

Fresh ginger is a wonderful spice, adding flavor as well as fire. Substituting the dried powdered ginger used in baking is out of the question. The fresh or "green" root is sold in food stores everywhere, however, and your only problem may be identifying it. It is quite small and very knobbly, similar to a Jerusalem artichoke in shape and color, and it should feel firm to the touch.

When the root is peeled, the yellow flesh is revealed and the delicious aroma wafts out. Ginger is usually grated and thrown into the wok at the start of cooking a stir-fry, infusing the oil with its wonderful flavor.

Garlic, crushed or chopped, is used throughout the world, and not just for spicy cooking, so fresh garlic is usually readily available. It is a bulb formed of edible cloves packed tightly around an inedible core. Garlic's reputation for tainting the breath is unfortunately entirely justified, but you may decide that the special flavor and subtle kick it imparts is worth it—chewing parsley or caraway seeds is said to reduce the odor.

Cooking Utensils

There is no essential piece of equipment needed for hot and spicy cuisine—your usual cooking pans and a good heavy skillet will be all you need—but if you intend to do a lot of spicy cooking, a wok is a very useful item of equipment to have in the kitchen. The wok is a Chinese cooking pan. It is shallow and convex in shape, allowing the heat to spread evenly, especially if it sits on a "collar" over the heat source. It is ideal for stir-frying because the curved sides make it easy to toss food as it cooks. For this you need a spatula with a long wooden handle to insulate your hand from the heat.

Although they are pricey, it is worth investing in a cast-iron wok, because these are most effective at retaining heat—and fast cooking is the key to successful stir-frying.

The wok is at its best when well seasoned. To do this, wipe it inside and out with oil, then bring it up to a high temperature in an oven or on a stove. Repeat this a few times to coat it well. The seasoned wok will then only need to be wiped after use, then cleaned with detergent and water and dried immediately to prevent rusting.

KEY	
	Simplicity level 1 – 3 (1 easiest, 3 slightly harder)
	Preparation time
	Cooking time

Caribbean Seafood Soup

This pretty green soup is packed with exotic flavors. The traditional local tuberous vegetables are replaced here with potato.

NUTRITIONAL INFORMATION

Calories	106	Sugars	. . . . .4g
Protein	. . . . .14g	Fat	. . . . .1g
Carbohydrate	. . . .11g	Saturates	. . . . .0.1g

🕒 30 mins   🕐 50 mins

SERVES 4–6

INGREDIENTS

5½ oz/150 g peeled medium shrimp

7 oz/200 g skinless firm white fish fillets, cubed

¾ tsp ground coriander

¼ tsp ground cumin

1 tsp chili paste, or to taste

3 tbsp fresh lemon juice, or to taste

1 tbsp butter

1 onion, halved and thinly sliced

2 large leeks, thinly sliced

3 garlic cloves, chopped finely

1 large potato, diced

5 cups chicken or vegetable bouillon

9 oz/250 g spinach leaves

½ cup coconut milk

salt and pepper

1 Put the shrimp and fish in a bowl with the coriander, cumin, chili paste, and lemon juice, and let it marinate.

2 Melt the butter in a large pan over a medium heat. Add the onion and leeks, cover, and cook for about 10 minutes, stirring occasionally, until they are soft. Add the garlic and cook for an additional 3–4 minutes.

3 Add the potato and bouillon. Bring to the boil, reduce the heat, cover, and cook gently for 15–20 minutes until the potato is tender. Stir in the spinach and continue cooking, uncovered, for about 3 minutes until the leaves have just wilted.

4 Cool slightly, then purée the mixture until smooth in a blender or a food processor.

5 Return the soup to the pan and stir in the coconut milk. Add the fish and shrimp with their marinade. Simmer gently for about 8 minutes, stirring frequently, until the fish is cooked and flakes easily.

6 Taste and adjust the seasoning, adding more chili paste and/or lemon juice if wished. Ladle the soup into warm bowls and serve very hot.

VARIATION
Add a handful of cilantro to the soup with the spinach for an authentic Caribbean flavor.

Spicy Lamb Soup

This thick and hearty main-course soup is bursting with exotic flavors and aromas. It is flavored with harissa, a hot spice mixture.

NUTRITIONAL INFORMATION

Calories 323	Sugars 6g
Protein 27g	Fat 13g
Carbohydrate . . .25g	Saturates 4g

40 mins   1hr 35 mins

SERVES 4–5

INGREDIENTS

1–2 tbsp olive oil

1 lb/450 g lean boneless lamb, such as shoulder or neck fillet, trimmed of fat and cut into ½ inch/1 cm cubes

1 onion, chopped finely

2-3 garlic cloves, crushed

5 cups water

14 oz/400 g canned chopped tomatoes in juice

1 bay leaf

½ tsp dried thyme

½ tsp dried oregano

⅛ tsp ground cinnamon

¼ tsp ground cumin

¼ tsp ground turmeric

1 tsp harissa, or more to taste

14 oz/400 g canned garbanzo beans, rinsed and drained

1 carrot, diced

1 potato, diced

1 zucchini, quartered lengthwise and sliced

3½ oz/100 g fresh or defrosted frozen green peas

chopped fresh mint or cilantro, to garnish

1 Heat the oil in a large pan or a cast-iron casserole over a medium-high heat. Add the lamb, in batches if necessary to avoid crowding the pan, and cook until it is evenly browned on all sides, adding a little more oil as needed. Remove the meat from the pan with a slotted spoon when it is browned.

2 Reduce the heat and add the onion and garlic to the pan. Cook, stirring frequently, for 1–2 minutes.

3 Add the water and return all the meat to the pan. Bring just to the boil and skim off any foam that rises to the surface. Reduce the heat and stir in the tomatoes, bay leaf, thyme, oregano, cinnamon, cumin, turmeric, and harissa. Simmer for about 1 hour, or until the meat is very tender. Discard the bay leaf.

4 Stir in the garbanzo beans, carrot and potato and simmer for 15 minutes. Add the zucchini and peas, and continue simmering for 15–20 minutes, or until all the vegetables are tender.

5 Adjust the seasoning, adding more harissa, if desired. Ladle the soup into warm bowls, garnish with mint or cilantro, and serve very hot.

Spicy Gazpacho

This classic Spanish cold soup is given a Mexican twist in this recipe by adding chiles and cilantro. Serve it with chunks of crusty bread.

NUTRITIONAL INFORMATION

Calories 125   Sugars 10g

Protein . . . . .3g   Fat 8g

Carbohydrate . . . .11g   Saturates 1g

30 mins, plus
2 hrs chilling   0 mins

SERVES 4–6

INGREDIENTS

1 cucumber

2 green bell peppers

6 ripe flavorful tomatoes

½ hot chile

½–1 onion, chopped finely

3–4 garlic cloves, chopped

4 tbsp extra-virgin olive oil

¼–½ tsp ground cumin

2–4 tsp sherry vinegar, or a combination of balsamic vinegar and wine vinegar

4 tbsp chopped cilantro

2 tbsp chopped fresh parsley

1¼ cups vegetable or chicken bouillon

2½ cups tomato juice or canned crushed tomatoes

salt and pepper

ice cubes, to serve

1 Cut the cucumber in quarters lengthwise. Remove the seeds with a teaspoon, then dice the flesh. Cut the bell peppers in half, remove the cores and seeds, then dice the flesh.

2 Skin the tomatoes: place in a bowl, cover with boiling water and stand for 30 seconds. Drain and plunge into cold water. Slide off the skins. Cut the tomatoes in half, deseed if wished, then chop the flesh. Carefully deseed the chile and then chop finely.

3 Combine half the cucumber, the bell pepper, tomatoes, and onion in a blender or a food processor with all the chile, garlic, olive oil, cumin, vinegar, cilantro, and parsley. Process with enough bouillon for a smooth purée.

4 Pour the puréed soup into a bowl and stir in the remaining bouillon and tomato juice. Add the remaining green pepper, cucumber, tomatoes, and onion, stirring well. Season with salt and pepper to taste, then cover and chill in the refrigerator for a few hours.

5 Ladle into bowls and serve with ice cubes in each bowl.

Mexican Chipotle Chile Soup

This soup evolved from the food stalls that line the streets of Tlalpan, a suburb of Mexico City: avocado, chicken, and smoky chipotle chiles.

NUTRITIONAL INFORMATION

Calories	218	Sugars	. . . . .1g
Protein	. . . . .28g	Fat	. . . . .11g
Carbohydrate	. . . .2g	Saturates	. . . . . . .2g

15 mins   0 mins

SERVES 4

INGREDIENTS

6¼ cups chicken bouillon

2–3 garlic cloves, chopped finely

1–2 chipotle chiles, cut into very thin strips (see Cook's Tip)

1 avocado

lime or lemon juice, for tossing

3–5 scallions, sliced thinly

12–14 oz/350–400 g cooked chicken breast meat, torn, or cut into shreds or thin strips

2 tbsp chopped cilantro

TO SERVE

1 lime, cut into wedges

handful of tortilla chips (optional)

1 Place the bouillon in a large pan, with the garlic and the chipotle chiles, and bring it to a boil.

2 Meanwhile, cut the avocado in half around the pit. Twist apart, then remove the pit with a knife. Carefully peel away the skin, dice the flesh, and toss it gently in lime or lemon juice to prevent discoloration.

3 Arrange the scallions, chicken, avocado, and cilantro in the base of 4 soup bowls or in a large serving bowl.

4 Ladle the hot bouillon over the ingredients in the dish, and serve with wedges of lime and a handful of tortilla chips, if using.

COOK'S TIP
Chipotle chiles are smoked and dried jalapeño chiles and are available canned or dried.

Authentic Guacamole

Guacamole is at its best when it is freshly made. Serve it as a sauce with anything Mexican, or as a dip for raw vegetable sticks or tortilla chips.

NUTRITIONAL INFORMATION

Calories	212	Sugars	.........1g
Protein	.........2g	Fat	.........21g
Carbohydrate	....3g	Saturates	.......4g

 15 mins   0 mins

SERVES 4

INGREDIENTS

1 ripe tomato

2 limes

2–3 ripe small to medium avocados, or 1–2 large ones

¼–½ onion, chopped finely

pinch of ground cumin

pinch of mild chili powder

½–1 green chiles, such as jalapeño or serrano, deseeded and chopped finely

1 tbsp cilantro, chopped finely, plus extra for garnishing

salt (optional)

tortilla chips, to serve (optional)

1 Skin the tomato: place in a bowl, cover with boiling water and let stand for 30 seconds. Drain and plunge the tomato into cold water. The skin will then slide off easily. Cut in half, deseed, and chop the tomato flesh.

2 Squeeze the juice from the limes into a small bowl. Cut one avocado in half around the pit. Twist apart, then remove the pit with a knife. Carefully peel off the skin, dice the flesh and toss in the bowl of lime juice to prevent them from discoloring. Mash the avocados coarsely.

3 Add the onion, tomato, cumin, chili powder, chopped chiles, and chopped cilantro to the mashed avocados. If the guacamole is to be used as a dip for tortilla chips do not add salt. If it is to be used as a sauce, add salt to taste.

4 To serve the Guacamole as a dip, transfer it to a serving dish, garnish with the finely chopped cilantro, and serve it with tortilla chips for dipping.

COOK'S TIP

Try spooning Guacamole into soups, especially chicken or seafood, or spreading it into sandwiches on thick crusty rolls. Spoon guacamole over refried beans and melted cheese, then dig into it with salsa and crisp tortilla chips.

Hot & Sour Soup

Hot-and-sour mixtures are popular throughout the East, especially in Thailand. This soup typically has either shrimp or chicken added.

NUTRITIONAL INFORMATION

Calories 71   Sugars 0.1g
Protein . . . . .8g   Fat 4g
Carbohydrate . . . .1g   Saturates 0.1g

30 mins   25 mins

SERVES 4

INGREDIENTS

2 cups whole raw or cooked shrimp in their shells

1 tbsp vegetable oil

1 lemon grass stem, chopped coarsely

2 kaffir lime leaves, shredded

1 green chile, deseeded and chopped

5 cups chicken or fish bouillon

1 lime

1 tbsp Thai fish sauce

1 red bird-eye chile, deseeded and sliced thinly

1 scallion, sliced thinly

salt and pepper

1 tbsp finely chopped cilantro, to garnish

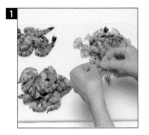

1 Peel the shrimp and reserve the shells. Devein the shrimp, cover, and chill.

2 Heat the oil in a large pan and stir-fry the shrimp shells for 3–4 minutes until they turn pink. Add the lemon grass, lime leaves, green chile, and bouillon. Grate the zest from the lime and add it.

3 Bring to the boil, then lower the heat, cover, and simmer the bouillon gently for about 20 minutes.

4 Strain the liquid and pour it back into the pan. Squeeze the juice from the lime and add to the pan with the fish sauce and salt and pepper to taste.

5 Bring the pan to a boil. Lower the heat, add the shrimp, and simmer for just 2–3 minutes.

6 Add the red chile and scallion. Sprinkle with cilantro and serve.

COOK'S TIP

To devein the shrimp, first remove the shells. Cut a slit along the back of each shrimp and remove the fine black vein that runs along the length of the back. Wipe each shrimp with clean paper towels.

Spinach & Ginger Soup

This mildly spiced, rich green soup is delicately scented with ginger and lemon grass. It makes a good light starter or a summer lunch dish.

NUTRITIONAL INFORMATION

Calories	38	Sugars	.......0.8g
Protein	........3.2g	Fat	.........1.8g
Carbohydrate	...2.4g	Saturates	.....0.2g

 15 mins   10 mins

SERVES 4

INGREDIENTS

2 tbsp sunflower oil

1 onion, chopped

2 garlic cloves, chopped finely

2 tsp fresh root ginger, chopped finely

9 oz/250 g fresh young spinach leaves

1 small lemon grass stem, chopped finely

1¾ pints/1 liter chicken or vegetable bouillon

8 oz/225 g potatoes, chopped small

1 tbsp rice wine or dry sherry

1 tsp sesame oil

salt and pepper

fresh spinach, shredded finely, to garnish

1 Heat the oil in a large pan. Add the onion, garlic, and ginger, and cook gently for 3–4 minutes until the onions are softened but not browned.

2 Add the spinach and lemon grass, stirring until the spinach is wilted. Add the bouillon and potatoes to the pan and bring to the boil. Lower the heat, cover, and simmer for about 10 minutes, until the potato is tender.

3 Tip the soup into a blender or a food processor, and process until it is completely smooth.

4 Return the soup to the pan and add the rice wine, then adjust the seasoning to taste with salt and pepper. Heat until just about to boil.

5 Drizzle with sesame oil and serve hot, garnished with the finely shredded fresh spinach leaves.

COOK'S TIP

To make a creamy-textured spinach and coconut soup, stir in 4 tablespoons of creamed coconut, or replace about 1¼ cups of the bouillon with coconut milk. Serve the soup scattered with shavings of fresh coconut.

Grilled Sesame Eggplant

Eggplants grow easily throughout the Far East and they are a popular vegetable in Thailand. This dish works well as a first course.

NUTRITIONAL INFORMATION

Calories	106	Sugars	.........6g
Protein	.........3g	Fat	...........8g
Carbohydrate	....7g	Saturates	.......1g

20 mins,   10 mins

SERVES 4

I N G R E D I E N T S

8 baby eggplants

salt

2 tsp chili oil

1 tbsp soy sauce

1 tbsp Thai fish sauce

1 garlic clove, sliced thinly

1 red bird-eye chile, deseeded and sliced

1 tbsp sunflower oil

1 tsp sesame oil

1 tbsp lime juice

1 tsp soft light brown sugar

1 tbsp fresh mint, chopped

1 tbsp sesame seeds, toasted

mint leaves, to garnish

1 Cut the eggplants lengthwise into thin slices to within 1 inch/2.5 cm of the stem end. Place the slices in a colander, sprinkling salt between them, and leave to drain for about 30 minutes. Rinse in cold water, then pat them completely dry with paper towels.

2 Mix the chili oil, soy sauce, and fish sauce, and brush over the eggplants. Cook under a hot broiler, or barbecue over hot coals, for 6–8 minutes, turning

occasionally and brushing with chili oil glaze, until golden and softened. Arrange the eggplants on a large serving platter.

3 Cook the sliced garlic and chile in the sunflower oil for 1–2 minutes until they just begin to brown. Remove the pan from the heat and place in it the sesame oil, lime juice, sugar, and any chili oil glaze you have left over.

4 Add the chopped mint and spoon the warm dressing over the eggplants.

5 Marinate for about 20 minutes, then sprinkle with toasted sesame seeds. Serve the dish garnished with mint.

Thai Fish Soup

This soup is also known as Tom Yam Gung. Oriental stores may sell ready-prepared tom yam sauce in jars, sometimes labelled "Chilis in Oil."

NUTRITIONAL INFORMATION

Calories	230	Sugars	.........4g
Protein	........22g	Fat	..........12g
Carbohydrate	....9g	Saturates	.......1g

  🕙 25 mins   ⏱ 5 mins

SERVES 4

INGREDIENTS

2 cups light chicken bouillon

2 lime leaves, chopped

2 inch/5 cm piece lemon grass, chopped

3 tbsp lemon juice

3 tbsp Thai fish sauce

2 small, hot green chiles, deseeded and chopped finely

½ tsp sugar

8 small shiitake mushrooms, halved

1 lb/450 g raw shrimp, peeled if necessary and deveined

scallions (shredded), to garnish

TOM YAM SAUCE

4 tbsp vegetable oil

5 garlic cloves, chopped finely

1 large shallot, chopped finely

2 large hot dried red chilis, chopped coarsely

1 tbsp dried shrimp (optional)

1 tbsp Thai fish sauce

2 tsp sugar

1 First make the tom yam sauce. Heat the oil in a small skillet. Cook the garlic for a few seconds until just brown. Remove with a slotted spoon and set aside. Cook the shallot in the oil until browned and crisp Remove, add the chilis, and cook until they darken. Remove and drain on paper towels. Remove the pan from the hob and save for later use.

2 In a food processor or a spice grinder, grind the dried shrimp, if using, then the reserved chilis, garlic, and shallot, to a smooth paste. Return to the original pan over a low heat. Mix in the fish sauce and sugar. Remove from the heat.

3 In a large pan, heat together the bouillon and 2 tablespoons of the tom yam sauce. Add the lime leaves, lemon grass, lemon juice, fish sauce, chiles, and sugar. Simmer for 2 minutes.

4 Add the mushrooms and shrimp, and cook a further 2–3 minutes until the shrimp are cooked. Ladle into warm bowls and serve immediately, garnished with the shredded scallions.

Thai Fish Cakes

These traditional Thai fish cakes are always accompanied by a hot, sweet, and sour dipping sauce. Remove the chile seeds for a milder sauce.

NUTRITIONAL INFORMATION

Calories	223	Sugars	........23g
Protein	........21g	Fat	...........4g
Carbohydrate	...25g	Saturates	.......1g

20 mins   6 mins

SERVES 4

I N G R E D I E N T S

1 lb/450 g firm white fish, skinned and chopped coarsely

1 tbsp Thai fish sauce

1 tbsp red curry paste

1 kaffir lime leaf, shredded finely

2 tbsp chopped cilantro

1 egg

1 tsp brown sugar

large pinch salt

1½ oz/40 g green beans, thinly sliced crosswise

vegetable oil, for shallow frying

DIPPING SAUCE

4 tbsp sugar

1 tbsp cold water

3 tbsp white rice vinegar

2 small, hot chiles, chopped finely

1 tbsp Thai fish sauce

1 For the fish cakes, put the fish, fish sauce, curry paste, lime leaf, cilantro, egg, sugar, and salt into the bowl of a food processor. Process until smooth. Scrape the mixture into a bowl, and stir in the green beans. Set aside.

2 To make the dipping sauce, heat the sugar, water, and rice vinegar gently in a small pan until the sugar is dissolved. Bring to a boil, simmer for 2 minutes, stir in the chiles and fish sauce, and leave to cool.

3 Heat a skillet with enough oil to cover the bottom generously. Divide the fish mixture into 16 little balls. Flatten the balls into patties and cook in the hot oil for 1–2 minutes each side until they are golden. Drain on paper towels. Serve hot with the dipping sauce.

COOK'S TIP
Use any firm white fish for this recipe, such as hake or haddock. The dish combines strong flavors, so you should use whatever fish is currently cheapest.

Indian Potato & Pea Soup

A slightly hot and spicy Indian flavor is given to this soup with the use of garam masala, chile, cumin, and coriander.

NUTRITIONAL INFORMATION

Calories 153	Sugars 6g
Protein 6g	Fat 6g
Carbohydrate ...18g	Saturates 1g

  15 mins 30 mins

SERVES 4

INGREDIENTS

2 tbsp vegetable oil

8 oz/225 g mealy potatoes, diced

1 large onion, chopped

2 garlic cloves, crushed

1 tsp garam masala

1 tsp ground coriander

1 tsp ground cumin

3¾ cups vegetable bouillon

1 red chile, chopped

3½ oz/100 g frozen peas

4 tbsp low-fat plain yogurt

salt and pepper

chopped cilantro, to garnish

COOK'S TIP

For slightly less heat, deseed the chile before adding it to the soup. Always wash your hands well after handling chiles as they contain volatile oils that can irritate the skin and make your eyes burn if you touch your face.

1 Heat the vegetable oil in a large pan and add the diced potatoes, onion, and garlic. Sauté gently for about 5 minutes, stirring constantly. Add the ground spices and cook for 1 minute, continuing to stir all the time.

2 Stir in the vegetable bouillon and the chopped red chile, and bring the mixture to a boil. Reduce the heat, cover the pan, and simmer for 20 minutes.

3 Add the frozen peas and cook for another 5 minutes. Stir in the yogurt and season as required to taste.

4 Pour the soup into warmed bowls, garnish with the chopped cilantro, and serve hot with warm crusty bread.

Vegetables with Sesame Dip

This tasty dip is great for livening up simply cooked vegetables. Varying the vegetables according to the season adds interest to the dish.

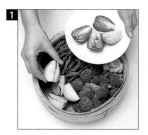  

NUTRITIONAL INFORMATION

Calories 126	Sugars 7g
Protein 11g	Fat 6g
Carbohydrate 8g	Saturates 1g

 5 mins   20 mins

SERVES 4

I N G R E D I E N T S

8 oz/225 g small broccoli florets

8 oz/225 g small cauliflower florets

8 oz/225 g asparagus, sliced into 2 inch/
  5 cm lengths

2 small red onions, quartered

1 tbsp lime juice

2 tsp toasted sesame seeds

1 tbsp chopped fresh chives, to garnish

HOT SESAME SEED PASTE & GARLIC DIP

1 tsp sunflower oil

2 garlic cloves, crushed

½–1 tsp chili powder

2 tsp sesame seed paste

⅔ cup low-fat plain yogurt

2 tbsp chopped fresh chives

salt and pepper

1 Line the base of a steamer with baking parchment and arrange the broccoli florets, cauliflower florets, asparagus, and onion pieces on top.

2 Bring a wok or large pot of water to a boil, and place the steamer on top. Sprinkle the vegetables with lime juice and steam them for 10 minutes, or until they are just tender.

3 To make the Hot Sesame Seed Paste & Garlic Dip, heat the oil in a small non-stick pan, add the garlic, chili powder, and seasoning to taste, and cook gently for 2–3 minutes until the garlic is softened.

4 Remove the pan from the heat and stir in the sesame seed paste and yogurt. Return the pan to the heat and cook gently for 1–2 minutes without bringing to a boil. Stir in the chives.

5 Remove the vegetables from the steamer and place on a warmed serving platter. Sprinkle them with the sesame seeds and garnish with chopped chives. Serve with the hot dip.

Thai-Style Burgers

If your family likes to eat burgers, try these—they have a much more interesting flavor than conventional hamburgers.

NUTRITIONAL INFORMATION

Calories	358	Sugars	.........1g
Protein	........23g	Fat	..........29g
Carbohydrate	....2g	Saturates	.......5g

15 mins   8 mins

SERVES 4

INGREDIENTS

1 small lemon grass stem

1 small red chili, deseeded

2 garlic cloves, peeled

2 scallions

2½ cups closed-cup mushrooms

14 oz/400 g ground pork

1 tbsp Thai fish sauce

3 tbsp chopped cilantro

sunflower oil for shallow frying

2 tbsp mayonnaise

1 tbsp lime juice

salt and pepper

TO SERVE

4 sesame hamburger buns

shredded Napa cabbage

1 Place the lemon grass, chili, garlic, and scallions in a food processor and process to a smooth paste. Add the mushrooms to the food processor and process until they are chopped very finely.

2 Add the ground pork, fish sauce, and cilantro. Season well with salt and pepper, then divide the mixture into 4 equal portions and shape with lightly floured hands into flat burger shapes.

3 Heat the oil in a skillet over a medium heat. Add the burgers to the pan and cook for 6–8 minutes until they are done to your taste.

4 Meanwhile, mix the mayonnaise with the lime juice. Split the hamburger buns and spread the lime-flavored mayonnaise on the cut surfaces. Add a few shredded Napa cabbage leaves, top with a burger, and sandwich together. Serve immediately, while still hot.

COOK'S TIP

Add a spoonful of your favorite relish to each burger or add a few pieces of crisp pickled vegetables for a change of texture.

Thai Rice Noodles

This quick and easy dish of noodles, mushrooms, and tofu is very filling.
If you omit the fish sauce, it can be served as a vegetarian dish.

NUTRITIONAL INFORMATION

Calories	361	Sugars	.........3g
Protein	.........9g	Fat	..........12g
Carbohydrate	...53g	Saturates	.......2g

5 mins, plus
15 mins soaking

5 mins

SERVES 4

I N G R E D I E N T S

8 oz/225 g rice stick noodles

2 tbsp vegetable oil

1 garlic clove, chopped finely

¾ inch/2 cm piece fresh ginger root,
   chopped finely

4 shallots, sliced thinly

¾ cup shiitake mushrooms, sliced

½ cup firm tofu, cut into ⅝ inch/1.5 cm dice

2 tbsp light soy sauce

1 tbsp rice wine

1 tbsp Thai fish sauce

1 tbsp smooth peanut butter

1 tsp chili sauce

2 tbsp toasted peanuts, chopped

shredded basil leaves, to serve

1 Soak the rice stick noodles in hot water for 15 minutes,
or according to the package directions. Drain well.

2 Heat the oil in a skillet or a wok and stir-fry the garlic,
ginger, and shallots for 1–2 minutes until they are
softened and lightly browned.

3 Add the mushrooms and continue to stir-fry for an
additional 2–3 minutes. Then stir in the tofu and toss
gently to brown lightly.

4 Mix together the soy sauce, rice wine, fish sauce,
peanut butter, and chili sauce, then stir into the pan.

5 Stir in the rice noodles and toss to coat evenly in
the sauce. Heat through, scatter with peanuts and
,shredded basil leaves and serve immediately.

COOK'S TIP

For an easy pantry dish, replace the
shiitake mushrooms with canned
Chinese straw mushrooms.
Alternatively, use dried shiitake
mushrooms, soaked and drained
before use.

Vegetables in Peanut Sauce

This colorful mix of vegetables in a rich, spicy peanut sauce may be served either as a side dish or as a vegetarian main course.

NUTRITIONAL INFORMATION

Calories 249	Sugars 10g	
Protein 10g	Fat 17g	
Carbohydrate . . .12g	Saturates 3g	

 10 mins   10 mins

SERVES 4

INGREDIENTS

2 carrots, peeled

1 small head cauliflower, trimmed

2 small heads green bok choy

5½ oz/150 g green beans, topped and tailed, if wished

2 tbsp vegetable oil

1 garlic clove, chopped finely

6 scallions, sliced

1 tsp chili paste

2 tbsp soy sauce

2 tbsp rice wine

4 tbsp smooth peanut butter

3 tbsp coconut milk

1 Cut the carrots diagonally into thin slices. Cut the cauliflower into small florets, then slice the stem thinly. Slice the bok choy thickly. Cut the beans into 1¼ inch/3 cm lengths.

2 Heat the oil in a large skillet or wok and stir-fry the garlic and scallions for 1 minute. Stir in the chili paste and cook for a few seconds.

3 Add the carrots and cauliflower and stir-fry for 2–3 minutes.

4 Add the bok choy and beans and stir-fry for a further 2 minutes.

5 Mix the soy sauce, rice wine, peanut butter, and coconut milk, and stir into the pan. Cook, stirring, for an additional minute. Serve immediately.

COOK'S TIP

It is important to cut the vegetables thinly and into even-sized pieces so they cook quickly and evenly. Prepare them all before you start to cook.

Spiced Cashew Nut Curry

This unusual vegetarian dish may be served on its own with rice, but is best presented as a side dish with other vegetable or meat.

NUTRITIONAL INFORMATION

Calories . . . . . . .455 Sugars 6g
Protein . . . . .13g Fat 39g
Carbohydrate . . .16g Saturates 11g

 15 mins, plus
12 hrs soaking   20 mins

SERVES 4

I N G R E D I E N T S

1½ cups unsalted cashew nuts

1 tsp coriander seeds

1 tsp cumin seeds

2 cardamom pods, crushed

1 tbsp sunflower oil

1 onion, finely sliced

1 garlic clove, crushed

1 small green chile, deseeded and chopped

1 cinnamon stick

½ tsp ground turmeric

4 tbsp coconut cream

1¼ cups hot vegetable bouillon

3 kaffir lime leaves, finely shredded

salt and pepper

boiled jasmine rice, to serve

1 Soak the cashew nuts in cold water overnight. Drain thoroughly. Crush the coriander seeds, cumin seeds, and cardamom pods in a spice grinder or with a pestle and mortar.

2 Heat the oil in a large skillet and stir-fry the onion and garlic for 2–3 minutes until they are soft but not brown. Add the chopped chile, crushed spices, cinnamon stick, and ground turmeric, and stir-fry for an additional minute.

3 Add the coconut cream and the hot bouillon to the pan. Bring to a boil, then add the cashew nuts and lime leaves, and salt and pepper to taste.

4 Cover the pan, lower the heat, and simmer for about 20 minutes. Serve hot, accompanied by jasmine rice.

COOK'S TIP
You can can always use ready-ground spices for speed, but all spices will give a better flavor if you crush them just before use in a spice grinder or with a pestle and mortar.

Thai Crab Omelet

Do not be put off by the long list of ingredients. This Thai omelet is served cold and so you can make it well in advance of its serving time.

NUTRITIONAL INFORMATION

Calories 262   Sugars 5g
Protein ....18g   Fat 19g
Carbohydrate ....5g   Saturates 7g

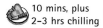 10 mins, plus 2–3 hrs chilling   10 mins

SERVES 4

I N G R E D I E N T S

8 oz/225 g white crab meat, fresh or thawed if frozen

3 scallions, chopped finely

1 tbsp chopped cilantro

1 tbsp chopped fresh chives

pinch cayenne pepper

2 tbsp vegetable oil

2 garlic cloves, crushed

1 tsp freshly grated ginger root

1 red chile, deseeded and chopped finely

2 tbsp lime juice

2 lime leaves, shredded

2 tsp sugar

2 tsp Thai fish sauce

3 eggs, lightly beaten

4 tbsp coconut cream

1 tsp salt

scallion slivers, to garnish

COOK'S TIP

You can also serve this omelet warm. After adding the crab, cook for 3–4 minutes to allow the mixture to heat through, then serve immediately.

1 Put the crab meat into a bowl and check for and remove any small pieces of shell. Add the scallions, cilantro, chives, and cayenne, and set aside.

2 Heat half the oil in a pan, and add the garlic, ginger, and chile, and stir-fry for 30 seconds. Add the lime juice, lime leaves, sugar, and fish sauce. Simmer for 3–4 minutes. Let the mixture cool, then add to the crab mixture and set it aside.

3 Beat the eggs, coconut cream, and salt lightly together. In a skillet, heat the remaining oil over a medium heat. Add the egg mixture and cook the omelet.

4 Spoon the crab mixture down the center of the omelet. Fold the omelet over the filling and turn out of the pan. Cool, then refrigerate for 2–3 hours. To serve, slice the omelet into four pieces and garnish with scallion slivers.

Kedgeree

Originally, kedgeree or *khichri* was a Hindi dish of rice and lentils, varied with fish or meat in all kinds of ways.

NUTRITIONAL INFORMATION

Calories	290	Sugars	.........7g
Protein	........27g	Fat	...........11g
Carbohydrate	...23g	Saturates	.......1g

 15 mins   35 mins

SERVES 4

I N G R E D I E N T S

1 lb/450 g undyed smoked haddock fillet

2 tbsp olive oil

1 large onion, chopped

2 garlic cloves, chopped finely

½ tsp ground turmeric

½ tsp ground cumin

1 tsp ground coriander

¾ cup basmati rice

4 medium eggs

2 tbsp butter

1 tbsp chopped fresh parsley

T O   S E R V E

lemon wedges

mango chutney

1 Pour boiling water over the haddock fillet and stand for 10 minutes. Lift the fish from the cooking water, discard the skin and bones, and flake the fish. Set aside. Reserve the cooking water.

2 Heat the oil in a large pan and add the onion. Cook for 10 minutes over a medium heat until it starts to brown. Add the garlic and cook for another 30 seconds. Add the turmeric, cumin, and coriander, and stir-fry the mixture for 30 seconds until the spices smell fragrant. Add the rice and stir well.

3 Measure 1½ cups of the haddock cooking water and add this to the pan. Stir well and bring to a boil. Cover and cook over a very low heat for 12–15 minutes until the rice is tender and all the bouillon is absorbed.

4 Meanwhile, bring a small pan of water to a boil and add the eggs. When the water has returned to a boil cook the eggs for 8 minutes. Immediately drain the eggs and refresh them under cold water to stop them cooking. Shell and quarter the boiled eggs.

5 Add the reserved fish pieces, the butter, and chopped parsley to the rice. Turn onto a large serving plate and garnish with the eggs. Serve with lemon wedges and mango chutney.

Chicken Tostadas

Chicken makes a delicate yet satisfying topping for crisp tostadas, served here with a fresh green salsa and smoky chipotle chiles.

NUTRITIONAL INFORMATION

Calories	663	Sugars	.........3g
Protein	........45g	Fat	..........32g
Carbohydrate	...49g	Saturates	......11g

15 mins   10 mins

SERVES 4–6

INGREDIENTS

6 corn tortillas

vegetable oil, for frying

1 lb/450 g skinned boned chicken breast or thigh, cut into strips or small pieces

1 cup chicken bouillon

2 garlic cloves, chopped finely

14 oz/400 g refried or canned Mexican beans

large pinch of ground cumin

2 cups grated cheese

1 tbsp chopped cilantro

2 ripe tomatoes, diced

handful of crisp salad greens, such as romaine or iceberg, shredded

4–6 radishes, diced

3 scallions, sliced thinly

1 ripe avocado (pitted), diced or sliced and tossed with lime juice

sour cream

1–2 canned chipotle chiles in adobo marinade, cut into thin strips

1 To make tostadas, cook the tortillas in a small amount of oil in a non-stick pan until crisp.

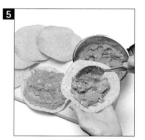

2 Put the chicken in a pan with the bouillon and garlic. Bring to a boil, then reduce the heat and cook for 1–2 minutes until the chicken begins to turn opaque.

3 Remove the pan from the heat and let the chicken steep in its hot liquid to cook through.

4 Heat the beans, adding a little water if necessary. Mash or blend in a food processor to form a smooth purée. Add the cumin and keep warm.

5 Reheat the tostadas under a preheated broiler, if necessary. Spread the hot bean purée on the tostadas, then sprinkle with the grated cheese. Lift the cooked chicken from the liquid, drain well, and divide between the tostadas. Top with the cilantro, tomatoes, salad greens, radishes, scallions, avocado, sour cream, and a few strips of chipotle. Serve the tostadas immediately.

Vegetable Tostadas

Top a crisp tostada with spicy vegetables, black beans, and feta cheese and you have a vegetarian feast.

NUTRITIONAL INFORMATION

Calories	.541	Sugars	.10g
Protein	.25g	Fat	.20g
Carbohydrate	.69g	Saturates	.9g

15 mins   20 mins

SERVES 4

INGREDIENTS

4 corn tortillas

vegetable oil, for frying

2–3 tbsp extra-virgin olive oil or
    vegetable oil

2 potatoes, diced

1 carrot, diced

3 garlic cloves, chopped finely

1 red bell pepper, deseeded and diced

1 tsp mild chili powder

1 tsp paprika

½ tsp ground cumin

3–4 ripe tomatoes, diced

4 oz/115 g green beans, blanched and cut
    into bite-size lengths

several large pinches dried oregano

14 oz/400 g cooked black beans, drained

8 oz/225 g crumbled feta cheese

3–4 leaves romaine lettuce, shredded

3–4 scallions, sliced thinly

1 To make tostadas, fry the tortillas in a small amount of oil in a non-stick pan until crisp.

2 Heat the olive oil in a skillet, add the potatoes and carrot, and cook until softened. Add the garlic, red bell pepper, chili powder, paprika, and cumin. Cook for 2–3 minutes until the pepper has softened.

3 Add the tomatoes, green beans, and oregano. Cook for 8–10 minutes until the vegetables are tender and form a sauce-like mixture. The mixture should not be too dry; add a little water if necessary, to keep it moist.

4 Preheat the broiler. Heat the black beans in a pan with a tiny amount of water, and keep warm. Reheat the tostadas under the broiler.

5 Layer the beans over the hot tostadas, then sprinkle with the cheese and top with a few spoonfuls of the hot vegetables in sauce. Serve at once, each tostada sprinkled with the lettuce and scallions.

Fragrant Black Bean Chili

Enjoy this chilied bean stew Mexican style with soft tortillas, or Californian style in a bowl with crisp tortilla chips crumbled in.

NUTRITIONAL INFORMATION

Calories	428	Sugars	........11g
Protein	........31g	Fat	..........10g
Carbohydrate	...53g	Saturates	.......2g

20 mins   2½ hrs

SERVES 4

INGREDIENTS

14 oz/400 g dried black beans, soaked overnight and drained

2 tbsp olive oil

1 onion, chopped

5 garlic cloves, coarsely chopped

2 slices bacon, diced (optional)

½–1 tsp ground cumin

½–1 tsp mild red chili powder

1 red bell pepper, diced

1 carrot, diced

14 oz/400 g tomatoes, canned and chopped, or fresh diced

1 bunch coarsely chopped, cilantro

salt and pepper

1 Put the beans in a pan, cover with water and bring to a boil. Boil for 10 minutes, then reduce the heat and simmer for about 1½ hours until tender. Drain well, reserving 1 cup of the cooking liquid.

2 Heat the oil in a skillet. Add the onion and garlic and cook for 2 minutes, stirring. Stir in the bacon, if using, and cook, stirring occasionally, until the bacon is cooked and the onion is soft.

3 Stir in the cumin and chili powder and cook for a few seconds. Add the red bell pepper, carrot, and tomatoes. Cook over a medium heat for 5 minutes.

4 Add half the cilantro and the beans and their reserved liquid. Season with salt and pepper. Simmer for 30–45 minutes or until thickened.

5 Stir through the remaining cilantro, adjust the seasoning to taste and serve at once.

COOK'S TIP

For speed you could use canned beans: drain off the liquid from the can and use 1 cup water for the liquid added in Step 4.

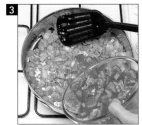

Migas

A wonderful brunch or late-night supper dish, this is made by scrambling egg with chiles, tomatoes, and crisp tortilla chips.

NUTRITIONAL INFORMATION

Calories	.441	Sugars	.5g
Protein	.22g	Fat	.20g
Carbohydrate	.46g	Saturates	.8g

 10 mins   10 mins

SERVES 4

INGREDIENTS

2 tbsp butter

6 garlic cloves, chopped finely

1 fresh green chile, such as jalapeño or serrano, deseeded and diced

1½ tsp ground cumin

6 ripe tomatoes, chopped coarsely

8 eggs, lightly beaten

8–10 corn tortillas, cut into strips and fried until crisp, or an equal amount of not too salty tortilla chips

4 tbsp chopped cilantro

3–4 scallions, sliced thinly

mild chili powder, to garnish

1 Melt half the butter in a pan. Add the garlic and chile and cook until softened but not browned. Add the cumin and cook for 30 seconds, stirring, then add the tomatoes and cook over a medium heat for an additional 3–4 minutes, or until the tomato juices have evaporated. Remove from the pan and set aside.

2 Melt the remaining butter in a skillet over a low heat and pour in the beaten eggs. Cook gently, stirring, until the egg begins to set.

3 Add the chile and tomato mixture, stirring gently to mix into the eggs.

4 Carefully add the tortilla strips or chips and continue cooking, stirring once or twice, until the eggs are the consistency you wish. The tortillas should be pliable and chewy.

5 Transfer the mixture to a serving plate and surround it with the chopped cilantro and sliced scallions. Garnish with a sprinkling of mild chili powder and serve immediately.

COOK'S TIP

Serve the migas with sour cream or crème fraîche on top, to melt seductively into the spicy eggs.

Potato-Filled Nans

This is a filling sandwich made with Indian bread. Spicy potatoes fill the nans, which are served with a cool cucumber raita and lime pickle.

NUTRITIONAL INFORMATION

Calories	244	Sugars	.........7g
Protein	.........8g	Fat	...........8g
Carbohydrate	...37g	Saturates	......1g

 10 mins   25 mins

SERVES 4

INGREDIENTS

8 oz/225 g waxy potatoes, scrubbed and diced

1 tbsp vegetable oil

1 onion, chopped

2 garlic cloves, crushed

1 tsp ground cumin

1 tsp ground coriander

½ tsp chili powder

1 tbsp tomato paste

3 tbsp vegetable bouillon

75 g/2¾ oz baby spinach, shredded

4 small or 2 large nans

lime pickle, to serve

RAITA

⅔ cup low-fat plain yogurt

4 tbsp diced cucumber

1 tbsp chopped mint

1 Cook the diced potatoes in a pan of boiling water for 10 minutes. Drain thoroughly.

2 Heat the vegetable oil in a separate pan and cook the onion and garlic for 3 minutes, stirring. Add the spices and cook for an additional 2 minutes.

3 Stir in the partially cooked potatoes, tomato paste, vegetable bouillon, and spinach. Cook for 5 minutes until the potatoes are tender.

4 Warm the nans in a preheated oven, 300°F/150°C, for about 2 minutes.

5 To make the raita, mix the yogurt, cucumber, and mint together in a small bowl.

6 Remove the nans from the oven. Using a sharp knife, cut a pocket in the side of each. Spoon some of the spicy potato mixture into each pocket.

7 Serve the filled nans at once, accompanied by the raita and lime pickle.

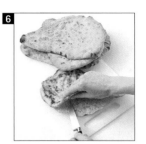

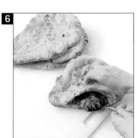

COOK'S TIP

To give the raita a much stronger flavor, make it in advance and leave it to chill in the refrigerator until you are ready to serve the meal.

Chicken Jalfrezi

This is a quick and tasty way of using leftover roast chicken. The sauce can also be used to accompany any cooked poultry, lamb, or beef.

NUTRITIONAL INFORMATION

Calories	.270	Sugars	.3g
Protein	.36g	Fat	.11g
Carbohydrate	.7g	Saturates	.2g

 25 mins   🕐 15 mins

SERVES 4

I N G R E D I E N T S

1 tsp mustard oil

3 tbsp vegetable oil

1 large onion, chopped finely

3 garlic cloves, crushed

1 tbsp tomato paste

2 tomatoes, skinned and chopped

1 tsp ground turmeric

½ tsp cumin seeds, ground

½ tsp coriander seeds, ground

½ tsp chili powder

½ tsp garam masala

1 tsp red wine vinegar

1 small red bell pepper, chopped

1 cup frozen fava beans

1 lb 2 oz/500 g cooked chicken, cut into bite-size pieces

salt

sprigs of cilantro, to garnish

1 Heat the mustard oil in a large skillet set over a high heat for about 1 minute until it begins to smoke.

2 Add the vegetable oil, reduce the heat, and then add the onion and the garlic. Cook them gently until they are softened and golden.

3 Add the tomato paste, chopped tomatoes, turmeric, ground cumin, and coriander seeds, chili powder, garam masala, and wine vinegar to the skillet. Stir the mixture over the heat until fragrant.

4 Add the red bell pepper and fava beans and stir for 2 minutes until the pepper is softened. Stir in the chicken, and add salt to taste.

5 Simmer gently for 6–8 minutes until the chicken is heated through and the beans are tender.

6 Serve immediately, garnished with sprigs of cilantro and accompanied by basmati rice.

Mixed Vegetable Balti

Any combination of vegetables or pulses can be used in this recipe. It would make a good dish to serve to vegetarians.

NUTRITIONAL INFORMATION

Calories 207	Sugars 6g
Protein 8g	Fat 9g
Carbohydrate . . .24g	Saturates 1g

 10 mins   1 hr 10 mins

SERVES 4

INGREDIENTS

1 cup split yellow peas, washed

3 tbsp oil

1 tsp onion seeds

2 onions, sliced

4½ oz/125 g zucchini, sliced

4½ oz/125 g potatoes, cut into
  ½ inch/1 cm cubes

4½ oz/125 g carrots, sliced

1 small eggplant, sliced

8 oz/225 g tomatoes, chopped

1¼ cups water

3 garlic cloves, chopped

1 tsp ground cumin

1 tsp ground coriander

1 tsp salt

2 fresh green chiles, sliced

½ tsp garam masala

2 tbsp chopped cilantro

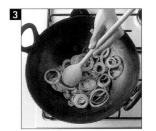

1 Put the split peas into a pan and cover with salted water. Bring to a boil and simmer for 30 minutes. Drain the peas and keep warm.

2 Heat the oil in a balti pan or a wok, and when it reaches a high heat, add the onion seeds. Keeping the heat high, cook them until they start popping.

3 Add the sliced onions and stir-fry until softened and golden brown.

4 Add the prepared zucchini, potatoes, carrots, and eggplant to the pan, and stir-fry for 2 minutes.

5 Stir in the chopped tomatoes, water, chopped garlic, ground cumin, ground coriander, salt, sliced chiles, garam masala, and the reserved split peas.

6 Bring to a boil, then simmer for 15 minutes until all the vegetables are tender, stirring from time to time.

7 Stir the cilantro into the vegetables and serve.

Meatballs in Spicy Sauce

These meatballs, flecked with cilantro, are delicious served with warm crusty bread to mop up the spicy tomato sauce.

NUTRITIONAL INFORMATION

Calories	95	Sugars 2.7g
Protein	. . . . .4.5g	Fat 5.8g
Carbohydrate	. . .6.6g	Saturates 2.3g

20 mins

1 hr 10 mins

SERVES 4

INGREDIENTS

8 oz/225 g mealy potatoes, diced

8 oz/225 g ground beef or lamb

1 onion, chopped finely

1 tbsp chopped cilantro

1 celery stalk, chopped finely

2 garlic cloves, crushed

2 tbsp butter

1 tbsp vegetable oil

salt and pepper

chopped cilantro, to garnish

SAUCE

1 tbsp vegetable oil

1 onion, finely chopped

2 tsp cornstarch

⅔ cup cold vegetable bouillon

2 tsp soft brown sugar

14 oz/400 g canned chopped tomatoes

1 green chile, chopped

1 tsp paprika

1 Cook the diced potatoes in boiling water for 10 minutes or until cooked through. Drain well and transfer to a large mixing bowl. Mash until smooth.

2 Add the ground beef or lamb, onion, cilantro, celery, and crushed garlic, and mix together well.

3 Bring the mixture together with your hands and roll it into 20 small balls.

4 To make the sauce, heat the oil in a pan and sauté the onion for 5 minutes. Put the cornstarch in a small bowl and very gradually stir in the bouillon. Add to the pan with the remaining sauce ingredients and bring to a boil, stirring constantly. Lower the heat and simmer the mixture for 20 minutes.

5 Meanwhile, heat the butter and oil for the meatballs in a skillet. Add the balls in batches and cook for 10–15 minutes until they are browned, turning frequently. Keep warm while cooking the remainder. Serve the meatballs in a warm, shallow, ovenproof dish with the sauce poured around them and garnished with the cilantro.

Spicy Lentils & Spinach

This is filling dish might be served with just a light main course or as a one-dish lunch or supper. Green split peas are a type of lentil.

NUTRITIONAL INFORMATION

Calories 355	Sugars 7g
Protein 20g	Fat 16g
Carbohydrate . . .35g	Saturates 2g

 10 mins, plus 2 hrs soaking   35 mins

SERVES 4

I N G R E D I E N T S

1¼ cups green split peas, washed

2 lb/900 g spinach

4 tbsp vegetable oil

1 onion, halved and sliced

1 tsp grated root ginger

1 tsp ground cumin

½ tsp chili powder

½ tsp ground coriander

2 garlic cloves, crushed

1¼ cups vegetable bouillon

salt and pepper

cilantro sprigs and lime wedges,
   to garnish

1 Rinse the peas under cold running water. Transfer to a mixing bowl, cover with cold water and let soak for 2 hours. Drain well.

2 Meanwhile, cook the spinach in a large pan for 5 minutes until wilted. Drain well and chop coarsely.

3 Heat the oil in a large pan and sauté the onion, spices and garlic. Sauté for 2–3 minutes, stirring well.

4 Add the split peas and spinach and stir in the bouillon. Cover and simmer for 10–15 minutes or until the split peas are cooked and the liquid has been absorbed. Season with salt and pepper to taste, garnish with sprigs of cilantro and wedges of lime to serve.

VARIATION
If you do not have time to soak the split peas, canned puy lentils (drained) are a good substitute.

Wild Mushroom Vermicelli

Simple to make, this spicy dish has Spanish chorizo sausage and anchovies as its main ingredients, and will set the taste buds tingling.

NUTRITIONAL INFORMATION

Calories 495	Sugars 1g	
Protein 15g	Fat 35g	
Carbohydrate ...33g	Saturates 5g	

 5 mins　　⏲ 10 mins

SERVES 6

INGREDIENTS

1½ lb/680 g dried vermicelli

½ cup olive oil

2 garlic cloves, chopped finely

4½ oz/125 g chorizo, sliced

8 oz/225 g wild mushrooms

3 fresh red chiles, chopped

2 tbsp freshly grated Parmesan cheese

salt and pepper

10 anchovy fillets, to garnish

1 Bring a large pan of lightly salted water to a boil. Add the vermicelli and 1 tbsp of the oil, and cook until just tender, but still firm to the bite. Drain, place on a large, warm serving plate, and keep warm.

2 Meanwhile heat the remaining oil in a large skillet. Add the garlic and cook for 1 minute. Add the chorizo and wild mushrooms and cook for 4 minutes, then add the chopped red chiles and cook for another minute, until the mushrooms are just cooked through.

3 Pour the chorizo and wild mushroom mixture over the vermicelli and season with a little salt and pepper. Sprinkle over freshly grated Parmesan cheese, garnish with a lattice of anchovy fillets and serve immediately.

COOK'S TIP
Always obtain wild mushrooms from a reliable source and never pick them yourself unless you are absolutely certain of their identity.

Stir-Fried Beef & Noodles

A quick-and-easy stir-fry for any day of the week, this is a good one-pan main dish. Serve a simple green side salad for a complete meal.

NUTRITIONAL INFORMATION

Calories . . . . . . .566 Sugars 9g
Protein . . . . .39g Fat 22g
Carbohydrate . . .55g Saturates 7g

10 mins   15 mins

SERVES 4

I N G R E D I E N T S

1 bunch scallions

2 tbsp sunflower oil

1 garlic clove, crushed

1 tsp fresh root ginger, chopped finely

1 lb 2 oz/500 g tender beef, cut into
    thin strips

1 large red bell pepper, deseeded
    and sliced

1 small red chile, deseeded and chopped

3⅓ cups fresh beansprouts

1 small lemon grass stem,
    chopped finely

2 tbsp smooth peanut butter

4 tbsp coconut milk

1 tbsp rice vinegar

1 tbsp soy sauce

1 tsp soft brown sugar

9 oz/250 g medium egg noodles

salt and pepper

1 Trim and thinly slice the scallions, setting aside some slices to use as a garnish.

2 Heat the oil in a skillet or wok over a high heat. Add the scallions, garlic, and ginger and then stir-fry for 2–3 minutes to soften. Add the beef and continue stir-frying for 4–5 minutes until browned evenly.

3 Add the bell pepper and stir-fry for another 3–4 minutes. Add the chile and beansprouts and stir-fry for 2 minutes. Mix together the lemon grass, peanut butter, coconut milk, vinegar, soy sauce, and sugar, then stir this mixture into the wok.

4 Meanwhile, cook the egg noodles in boiling, lightly salted water for 4 minutes, or according to the package directions. Drain and stir into the skillet or wok, tossing to mix evenly.

5 Season with salt and pepper to taste. Sprinkle with the reserved scallions and serve hot.

Red-Hot Beef with Cashews

Hot and spicy, these quickly cooked beef strips are very tempting. Serve them with lots of plain rice and cucumber slices to offset the fieriness.

NUTRITIONAL INFORMATION

Calories	257	Sugars	.........1g
Protein	........32g	Fat	..........13g
Carbohydrate	....3g	Saturates	.......4g

15 mins, plus 2 hrs marinating   8 mins

SERVES 4

INGREDIENTS

1 lb 2 oz/500 g boneless, lean beef sirloin, sliced thinly

1 tsp vegetable oil

MARINADE

1 tbsp sesame seeds

1 garlic clove, chopped

1 tbsp fresh ginger root, chopped finely

1 red bird-eye chile, chopped

2 tbsp dark soy sauce

1 tsp red curry paste

TO FINISH

1 tsp sesame oil

4 tbsp unsalted cashew nuts

1 scallion, thickly sliced diagonally

cucumber slices, to garnish

1 Cut the beef into ½ inch/1 cm wide strips. Place them in a large, non-metallic bowl.

2 To make the marinade, toast the sesame seeds in a heavy-based pan over a medium heat for 2–3 minutes until golden brown, shaking the pan occasionally.

3 Grind the garlic, ginger, and chile to a smooth paste with a pestle and mortar. Add the soy sauce and curry paste and mix well.

4 Spoon the paste over the beef strips and toss well to coat the meat evenly. Cover and leave to marinate in the refrigerator for 2–3 hours, or overnight.

5 Heat a heavy skillet or griddle until very hot and brush with vegetable oil. Add the beef strips and cook quickly, turning often, until lightly browned. Remove from the heat and spoon onto a hot serving dish.

6 Heat the sesame oil in a small pan and quickly cook the cashew nuts until golden. Take care that they do not burn. Add the scallions and stir-fry for 30 seconds. Sprinkle the mixture on top of the beef strips and serve immediately, garnished with cucumber slices.

Hot Beef & Coconut Curry

The heat of the chili in this curry is balanced and softened by the coconut milk, producing a creamy-textured, rich, and lavishly spiced dish.

NUTRITIONAL INFORMATION

Calories	230	Sugars	.........6g
Protein	........29g	Fat	..........10g
Carbohydrate	....8g	Saturates	.......3g

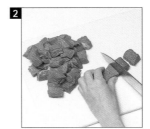 15 mins   ⏱ 40 mins

SERVES 4

I N G R E D I E N T S

1¾ cups coconut milk

2 tbsp Thai red curry paste

2 garlic cloves, crushed

1lb 2 oz/500 g braising steak

2 kaffir lime leaves, shredded

3 tbsp kaffir lime juice

2 tbsp Thai fish sauce

1 large red chile, deseeded and sliced

½ tsp turmeric

½ tsp salt

2 tbsp fresh basil leaves, chopped

2 tbsp cilantro leaves, chopped

shredded coconut, to garnish

boiled rice, to serve

1 Bring the coconut milk to a boil in a large pan. Lower the heat, then simmer gently for 10 minutes to thicken. Stir in the red curry paste and garlic, and simmer for an additional 5 minutes.

2 Cut the beef into ¾ inch/2 cm chunks, and add them to the pan. Bring the curry to a boil, stirring constantly, then lower the heat.

3 Add the lime leaves, lime juice, fish sauce, chile, turmeric, and salt. Cover the pan and simmer for 20–25 minutes until the meat is tender, adding a little water if the sauce looks too dry.

4 Stir in the fresh basil and cilantro, and adjust the seasoning to taste. Sprinkle the curry with coconut and serve immediately with boiled rice.

COOK'S TIP

This recipe uses one of the larger, milder red chile peppers—either fresno or Dutch—simply because they give more color to the dish. If you prefer to use small Thai, or bird-eye, chiles, you will still need only one because they are much hotter.

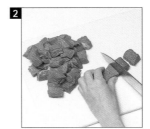

Red Lamb Curry

This curry uses the typically red-hot chili flavor of Thai red curry paste, made with dried red chilis, to give it a warm, russet color.

NUTRITIONAL INFORMATION

Calories	363	Sugars	........11g
Protein	........29g	Fat	..........19g
Carbohydrate	...21g	Saturates	.......6g

  15 mins 35–40 mins

SERVES 4

INGREDIENTS

1 lb 2 oz/500 g boneless lean leg of lamb

2 tbsp vegetable oil

1 large onion, sliced

2 garlic cloves, crushed

2 tbsp red curry paste

⅔ cup coconut milk

1 tbsp soft brown sugar

1 large red bell pepper, deseeded and sliced thickly

½ cup lamb or beef bouillon

1 tbsp Thai fish sauce

2 tbsp lime juice

8 oz/227 g canned water chestnuts, drained

2 tbsp chopped cilantro

2 tbsp chopped fresh basil

salt and pepper

boiled jasmine rice, to serve

fresh basil leaves, to garnish

1 Trim the meat and cut it into 1¼ inch/3 cm cubes. Heat the oil in a large skillet or wok over a high heat, and stir-fry the onion and garlic for 2–3 minutes. Add the meat and continue to stir-fry the mixture quickly over a high heat until the meat is lightly browned.

2 Stir in the curry paste and cook for a few seconds, then add the coconut milk and sugar and bring to a boil. Reduce the heat and simmer for 15 minutes, stirring the mixture occasionally.

3 Stir in the sliced red bell pepper, bouillon, Thai fish sauce, and lime juice. Cover the pan and continue simmering for another 15 minutes, or until the meat is tender.

4 Add the water chestnuts, chopped cilantro, and basil, and adjust the seasoning to taste. Serve immediately, accompanied by jasmine rice and garnished with fresh basil leaves.

Chicken & Mango Stir-Fry

A colorful, exotic mix of flavors that works surprisingly well, this dish is easy and quick to cook—ideal for a mid-week family meal.

NUTRITIONAL INFORMATION

Calories 200   Sugars 5g
Protein ....23g   Fat 6g
Carbohydrate ....7g   Saturates 1g

15 mins   15 mins

SERVES 4

INGREDIENTS

6 boneless, skinless chicken thighs

2 tsp grated fresh root ginger

1 garlic clove, crushed

1 small red chile, deseeded

1 large red bell pepper

4 scallions

7 oz/200 g snow peas

3½ oz/100 g baby corncobs

1 large, firm, ripe mango

2 tbsp sunflower oil

1 tbsp light soy sauce

3 tbsp rice wine or sherry

1 tsp sesame oil

salt and pepper

snipped chives, to garnish

1 Cut the chicken into long, thin strips and place in a bowl. Mix together the ginger, garlic, and chile, then stir into the chicken strips to coat them evenly.

2 Slice the red bell pepper thinly, cutting diagonally. Trim the carrots and slice them diagonally. Cut the snow peas and corncobs in half diagonally. Peel the mango, remove the pit, and slice thinly.

3 Heat the oil in a large skillet or wok over a high heat. Add the chicken and stir-fry for 4–5 minutes until just turning golden brown. Add the bell pepper and stir-fry over a medium heat for 4–5 minutes to soften.

4 Add the scallions, snow peas, and corncobs, and stir-fry for an additional minute.

5 Mix together the soy sauce, rice wine or sherry, and sesame oil, and stir into the wok. Add the mango and stir gently for 1 minute to heat thoroughly.

6 Adjust the seasoning with salt and pepper to taste, and serve immediately, garnished with chives.

Spiced Cilantro Chicken

These simple Thai-style marinated chicken breasts are packed with the powerful flavors of chile, ginger, lime, cilantro, and coconut.

NUTRITIONAL INFORMATION

Calories	171	Sugars	. . . . .8g
Protein	. . . . .31g	Fat	. . . . .2g
Carbohydrate	. . . .9g	Saturates	. . . . .1/2g

15 mins, plus 1hr marinating   15 mins

SERVES 4

INGREDIENTS

4 medium boneless, skinless chicken breasts

2 garlic cloves, peeled

1 green chile, deseeded

¾ inch/2 cm piece ginger root, peeled

4 tbsp chopped cilantro

zest of 1 lime, grated finely

3 tbsp lime juice

2 tbsp light soy sauce

1 tbsp superfine sugar

¾ cup coconut milk

plain boiled rice, to serve

cucumber and radish slices, to garnish

1 Using a sharp knife, cut 3 deep slashes into the skinned side of each chicken breast. Place the breasts in a single layer in a wide, non-metallic dish.

2 Put the garlic, chile, ginger, cilantro, lime zest and juice, soy sauce, superfine sugar, and coconut milk in a food processor and process to a smooth paste.

3 Spread the paste over both sides of the chicken breasts, coating them evenly. Cover the dish and marinate in the refrigerator for about 1 hour.

4 Lift the chicken from the marinade, drain off the excess, and place in a broiler pan. Broil under a preheated broiler for 12–15 minutes, turning, until thoroughly and evenly cooked.

5 Meanwhile, place the remaining marinade in a pan and bring to a boil. Lower the heat and simmer for several minutes to heat thoroughly. Serve with the chicken breasts, accompanied with rice, and garnish the dish with slices of cucumber and radish.

Green Chicken Curry

Thai curries are usually very hot and this one follows the tradition. Serve it with plenty of plain boiled rice to absorb the thin, highly spiced juices.

NUTRITIONAL INFORMATION

Calories 193	Sugars 9g
Protein 22g	Fat 8g
Carbohydrate 9g	Saturates 1g

15 mins   40 mins

SERVES 4

INGREDIENTS

6 boneless, skinless chicken thighs

1¾ cups coconut milk

2 garlic cloves, crushed

2 tbsp Thai fish sauce

2 tbsp Thai green curry paste

12 baby or Thai pea eggplants

3 green chiles, chopped finely

3 kaffir lime leaves, shredded

4 tbsp chopped cilantro

boiled rice, to serve

1 Cut the chicken into bite-size pieces. Pour the coconut milk into a large skillet or wok over a high heat, and bring to a boil. Add the chicken, garlic, and Thai fish sauce, and bring back to a boil.

COOK'S TIP

Baby eggplants, or "pea eggplants" as they are called in Thailand, are traditionally used in this curry, but they are not always easily available outside the country. If you cannot find baby eggplants in an Asian food shop, use chopped ordinary eggplant instead.

2 Lower the heat and simmer the ingredients gently for 30 minutes, or until the chicken is just tender. Stir the dish occasionally as it simmers.

3 Remove the chicken from the coconut mixture with a perforated spoon. Set aside and keep warm.

4 Stir the curry paste into the skillet, add the eggplants, chiles, and lime leaves, and simmer for 5 minutes.

5 Return the chicken to the skillet and bring to a boil. Adjust the seasoning to taste with salt and pepper, then stir in the cilantro. Serve with boiled rice.

Crispy Duck with Noodles

A robustly flavored dish that makes a substantial main course. Serve it with a refreshing cucumber salad or a light vegetable stir-fry.

NUTRITIONAL INFORMATION

Calories	433	Sugars	.........7g
Protein	........25g	Fat	..........10g
Carbohydrate	...59g	Saturates	.......2g

20 mins, plus 1hr marinating   30 mins

SERVES 4

INGREDIENTS

3 duck breasts, total weight about 14 oz/400 g

2 garlic cloves, crushed

1½ tsp chile paste

1 tbsp honey

3 tbsp dark soy sauce

½ tsp five-spice powder

9 oz/250 g rice stick noodles

1 tsp vegetable oil

1 tsp sesame oil

2 scallions, sliced

3½ oz/100 g snow peas

2 tbsp tamarind juice

sesame seeds, to garnish

1 Prick the duck breast skin all over with a fork and place in a deep dish.

2 Mix together the garlic, chile, honey, soy sauce, and five-spice powder, then pour over the duck breasts. Turn to coat evenly, then cover and marinate in the refrigerator for at least 1 hour.

3 Meanwhile, soak the rice noodles in hot water for 15 minutes. Drain well.

4 Drain the duck breasts from the marinade and broil on a rack under a high heat for about 10 minutes, turning them over occasionally, until they become a rich golden brown. Transfer the duck breasts to a plate, slice them thinly, and keep them warm until needed.

5 Heat the vegetable and sesame oils in a skillet, add the sliced scallions and the snow peas, and toss for 2 minutes. Stir in the reserved marinade and tamarind, and bring to a boil.

6 Add the sliced duck and noodles to the skillet, and toss to heat them thoroughly. Serve immediately, sprinkled with sesame seeds to garnish.

Rice Noodles with Chicken

The great thing about stir-fries is that you cook with very little fat, yet still produce a dish with plenty of flavor, as in this light lunch dish.

NUTRITIONAL INFORMATION

Calories	329	Sugars	.........3g
Protein	........25g	Fat	...........4g
Carbohydrate	...46g	Saturates	.......1g

  20 mins   🕐 20 mins

SERVES 4

I N G R E D I E N T S

7 oz/200 g rice stick noodles

1 tbsp sunflower oil

1 garlic clove, chopped finely

¾ inch/2 cm piece fresh root ginger, chopped finely

4 scallions, chopped

1 red bird-eye chile, deseeded and sliced

2 cups boneless, skinless chicken, chopped finely

2 chicken livers, chopped finely

1 celery stalk, sliced thinly

1 carrot, cut into short thin sticks

5½ cups shredded Napa cabbage

4 tbsp lime juice

2 tbsp Thai fish sauce

1 tbsp soy sauce

TO GARNISH

2 tbsp fresh mint, shredded

slices of pickled garlic

fresh mint sprig

1 Soak the rice noodles in hot water for 15 minutes, or according to the package directions. Drain well.

2 Heat the oil in a wok or a large skillet and stir-fry the garlic, ginger, scallions, and chile for 1 minute. Stir in the chicken and chicken livers, then stir-fry over a high heat for 2–3 minutes until they begin to brown.

3 Stir in the celery and carrot, and stir-fry for 2 minutes to soften. Add the Napa cabbage, then stir in the lime juice, Thai fish sauce, and soy sauce.

4 Add the noodles and stir to heat thoroughly. Sprinkle with shredded mint and pickled garlic. Serve immediately, garnished with a mint sprig.

Spicy Pork with Prunes

Prunes add an earthy, wine flavor to this spicy stew. Serve with tortillas or crusty bread to dip into the rich sauce.

NUTRITIONAL INFORMATION

Calories ...:....352 Sugars 1g
Protein ....39g Fat 12g
Carbohydrate ...24g Saturates 9g

15 mins, plus 8 hrs marinating

3 hrs 50 mins

SERVES 4–6

INGREDIENTS

3 lb 5 oz/1.5 kg pork joint, such as leg or shoulder

juice of 2–3 limes

10 garlic cloves, chopped

3–4 tbsp mild chili powder, such as ancho or New Mexico

4 tbsp vegetable oil

2 onions, chopped

2¼ cups chicken bouillon

25 small tart tomatoes, chopped coarsely

25 prunes, pitted

1–2 tsp sugar

pinch of ground cinnamon

pinch of ground allspice

pinch of ground cumin

salt

warmed corn tortillas, to serve

1 Combine the pork with the lime juice, garlic, chili powder, 2 tablespoons of oil, and salt. Let the mixture marinate in the refrigerator overnight.

2 Remove the pork from the marinade, wipe dry with paper towels, and keep the marinade. Heat the remaining oil in a flameproof casserole and brown the pork evenly until just golden. Add the onions, the reserved marinade, and the bouillon. Cover and cook in a preheated oven, 350°F/180°C, for 2–3 hours until tender.

3 Spoon off the fat from the surface of the cooking liquid and add the tomatoes. Continue to cook for 20 minutes or until the tomatoes are tender. Mash the tomatoes into a coarse paste. Add the prunes, sugar, and spices to taste.

4 Increase the oven temperature to 400°F/200°C. Cook the meat and sauce in the oven, uncovered, for 20–30 minutes, until the meat has browned and the juices have thickened.

5 Remove the meat from the pan and let it stand for a few minutes, carve into thin slices, and spoon the sauce over the top. Serve warm, with tortillas.

Chicken with Vinegar

Roasted garlic and mixed spices give an evocative flavor to this tangy chicken dish, a speciality of Valladolid in the Yucatan peninsula.

NUTRITIONAL INFORMATION

Calories 313	Sugars 6g	
Protein 15g	Fat 22g	
Carbohydrate . . .14g	Saturates 3g	

🐾 🐾 🐾

🍲 20 mins, plus
1 hr marinating   🕐 25 mins

SERVES 4

I N G R E D I E N T S

8 small boned chicken thighs

chicken bouillon

15–20 garlic cloves, unpeeled

1 tsp coarsely ground black pepper

½ tsp ground cloves

2 tsp crumbled dried oregano or ½ tsp crushed or powdered bay leaves

about ½ tsp salt

1 tbsp lime juice

1 tsp cumin seeds, lightly toasted

1 tbsp flour, plus extra for dredging the chicken

3–4 onions, sliced thinly

2 chiles, preferably mildish yellow ones, such as Mexican Guero or similar Turkish or Greek chiles, deseeded and sliced

1 cup vegetable oil

scant ½ cup cider or sherry vinegar

1 Place the chicken in a pan with enough bouillon to cover. Bring to a boil, then reduce the heat and simmer for 5 minutes. Remove from the heat, allow the chicken to cool, and continue to cook in the bouillon.

2 Meanwhile, roast the garlic cloves in a dry skillet until they are lightly browned on all sides and tender inside. Cool, then squeeze the flesh from the skins.

3 Grind the garlic, pepper, cloves, oregano, salt, lime juice, and ¾ teaspoon of the cumin seeds. Add the flour.

4 When the chicken is cool, remove from the bouillon and pat dry. Reserve the bouillon. Rub the chicken with about two-thirds of the garlic-spice paste, and marinate for 1–12 hours in the refrigerator.

5 Fry the onions and chiles in a little oil until golden brown. Pour in the vinegar and remaining cumin seeds, cook for a few minutes, then add the reserved bouillon and remaining spice paste. Boil, stirring, for 10 minutes.

6 Dredge the chicken in flour. Fry in oil until lightly browned. Serve with the onion mixture.

Ginger Beef with Chili

Serve these fruity, hot and spicy steaks with noodles. Use a non-stick ridged skillet to cook with a minimum of fat.

NUTRITIONAL INFORMATION

Calories ....179 Sugars 8g
Protein ....21g Fat 6g
Carbohydrate ....8g Saturates 2g

15 mins, plus 30 mins marinating   10 mins

SERVES 4

I N G R E D I E N T S

4 lean beef steaks (such as rump, sirloin or fillet), 3½ oz/100 g each

2 tbsp ginger wine

1 inch/2.5 cm piece fresh root ginger, chopped finely

1 garlic clove, crushed

1 tsp ground chili

1 tsp vegetable oil

salt and pepper

red chile strips, to garnish

TO SERVE

freshly cooked noodles

2 scallions, shredded

relish

8 oz/225 g fresh pineapple

1 small red bell pepper

1 red chile

2 tbsp light soy sauce

1 piece stem ginger in syrup, drained and chopped

1 Trim any excess fat from the beef if necessary. Using a meat mallet or covered rolling pin, pound the steaks until they are approximately ½ inch/1 cm thick. Season on both sides and place in a shallow dish.

2 Mix the ginger wine, chopped finely ginger, garlic, and chile and pour over the meat. Cover and marinate, chilled, for 30 minutes.

3 Meanwhile, make the relish. Peel and finely chop the pineapple and place it in a bowl. Halve, deseed, and chop the bell pepper and chile finely. Stir into the pineapple together with the soy sauce and stem ginger. Cover and chill until required.

4 Brush a broiler pan with the oil and heat until very hot. Drain the steaks and add to the pan, pressing down to seal. Lower the heat and cook for 5 minutes. Turn the steaks over and cook for an additional 5 minutes.

5 Drain the steaks on paper towels and transfer to serving plates. Garnish with chile strips, and serve with noodles, scallions, and the relish.

Chicken with a Yogurt Crust

A spicy, Indian-style coating is baked around lean chicken to give a full flavor. Serve with a tomato, cucumber, and cilantro relish.

NUTRITIONAL INFORMATION

Calories 176	Sugars 5g	
Protein 30g	Fat 4g	
Carbohydrate 5g	Saturates 1g	

🍗 🕐

🍲 10 mins   🕐 35 mins

SERVES 4

INGREDIENTS

1 garlic clove, crushed

1 inch/2.5 cm piece fresh root ginger, chopped finely

1 fresh green chile, deseeded and chopped finely

6 tbsp low-fat plain yogurt

1 tbsp tomato paste

1 tsp ground turmeric

1 tsp garam masala

1 tbsp lime juice

4 medium boneless, skinless chicken breasts

salt and pepper

wedges of lime or lemon, to serve

RELISH

4 medium tomatoes

¼ cucumber

1 small red onion

2 tbsp fresh chopped cilantro

1 Preheat the oven to 375°F/190°C. Place the garlic, ginger, chile, yogurt, tomato paste, spices, lime juice, and seasoning in a bowl, and mix to combine.

2 Wash the chicken, dry with paper towels, and place on a cookie sheet.

3 Brush or spread the spicy yogurt mix over the chicken, and bake in the oven for 30–35 minutes until the meat is tender and cooked through.

4 Meanwhile, make the relish. Chop the tomatoes, cucumber, and red onion finely, and mix together with the cilantro. Season with salt and pepper to taste, cover with plastic wrap, and chill in the refrigerator until required.

5 Serve the chicken breasts hot with the relish and lemon or lime wedges. Alternatively, let cool and chill for at least 1 hour and serve sliced as part of a salad.

Barbecued Indian Chicken

This Indian-influenced barbecue dish is delicious on a warm evening, served with warm nan and a cool, fresh cucumber raita.

NUTRITIONAL INFORMATION

Calories	228	Sugars	........12g
Protein	........28g	Fat	...........8g
Carbohydrate	...12g	Saturates	......2g

20 mins   10 mins

SERVES 4

I N G R E D I E N T S

4 medium boneless, skinless chicken breasts

2 tbsp curry paste

1 tbsp sunflower oil

1 tbsp brown sugar

1 tsp ground ginger

½ tsp ground cumin

TO SERVE

warm nan

green salad leaves

CUCUMBER RAITA

¼ cucumber

salt

⅔ cup low-fat plain yogurt

¼ tsp chili powder

1 Place the chicken breasts between 2 sheets of baking parchment or plastic wrap. Flatten them with a meat mallet or a rolling pin.

2 Mix the curry paste, oil, sugar, ginger, and cumin in a small bowl. Spread the mixture over both sides of the chicken and set aside until required.

3 To make the raita, peel the cucumber and scoop out the seeds with a spoon. Grate the cucumber flesh, sprinkle with salt, place in a sieve, and let stand for 10 minutes. Rinse off the salt and squeeze out any moisture. Mix with the yogurt and the chili powder. Chill until required.

4 Transfer the chicken to an oiled rack and barbecue over hot coals for 10 minutes, turning once. Serve with warm nans, raita, and green salad leaves.

Lamb Couscous

Couscous is a North African speciality. It is usually accompanied by a spicy mixture of meat or sausage and fruit which add a note of luxury.

NUTRITIONAL INFORMATION

Calories 647   Sugars 22g
Protein ....41g   Fat 21g
Carbohydrate ...79g   Saturates 6g

   20 mins   20 mins

SERVES 4

INGREDIENTS

2 tbsp olive oil

1 lb 2 oz/500 g lean lamb tenderloin, sliced thinly

2 onions, sliced

2 garlic cloves, chopped

1 cinnamon stick

1 tsp ground ginger

1 tsp paprika

½ tsp chili powder

2½ cups hot chicken bouillon

3 carrots, sliced thinly

2 turnips, halved and sliced

14 oz/400 g canned chopped tomatoes

2 tbsp raisins

15 oz/425 g canned garbanzo beans, drained and rinsed

3 zucchini, sliced

4½ oz/125 g fresh dates, halved and pitted or 4½ oz/125 g dried apricots

1¾ cups couscous

2½ cups boiling water

salt

1 Heat the oil in a skillet and cook the lamb briskly for 3 minutes until browned. Remove from the skillet with a perforated spoon, and set aside.

2 Add the onions to the pan and cook, stirring constantly, until soft. Add the garlic and spices and cook for 1 minute.

3 Add the bouillon, carrots, turnips, tomatoes, raisins, garbanzo beans, lamb, and salt to taste. Cover, bring to a boil, and simmer for 12 minutes.

4 Add the zucchini and the dates. Cover again and cook for 8 minutes.

5 Meanwhile, put the couscous in a bowl with 1 teaspoon of salt and pour the boiling water over it. Let it soak for 5 minutes, then fluff it with a fork.

6 To serve, pile the couscous onto a warmed serving platter and make a hollow in the centre. Put the meat and vegetables in the hollow, and pour some of the sauce over it. Serve the rest of the sauce separately.

Masala Lamb & Lentils

This recipe makes a hearty, warming winter curry. Gram lentils are used in this recipe but split yellow peas make a tasty alternative.

NUTRITIONAL INFORMATION

Calories	397	Sugars	.........1g
Protein	........42g	Fat	..........22g
Carbohydrate	....8g	Saturates	......9g

20 min, plus 6 hrs soaking

1¼ hrs

SERVES 4

INGREDIENTS

2 tbsp oil

1 tsp cumin seeds

2 bay leaves

1 inch/2.5 cm piece cinnamon stick

1 onion, chopped

1 lb 10 oz/750 g lean, boneless lamb, cut into 1 inch/2.5 cm cubes

½ cup split gram lentils, soaked for 6 hours and drained

1 tsp salt

1 fresh green chile, sliced

5 cups water

1 garlic clove, crushed

¼ tsp ground turmeric

1 tsp chili powder

½ tsp garam masala or curry powder (optional)

1 tbsp chopped cilantro (optional)

1 Heat the oil in a balti pan or a wok, add the cumin seeds, bay leaves, and cinnamon stick, and cook over a high heat until the cumin seeds start popping.

2 Add the onion to the pan and stir-fry until golden brown. Stir the lamb into the balti pan or wok, and stir-fry until evenly browned.

3 Add the lentils, salt, chile, water, garlic, turmeric, and chili powder, and stir well to combine all the ingredients Bring the mixture to a boil, and simmer for 1 hour, stirring occasionally.

4 Season with garam masala and cook for another 5 minutes.

5 Stir in the chopped cilantro, if using, and serve with nans and pickles.

COOK'S TIP

To save time on soaking, use 14 oz/400 g canned lentils. These should be added to the curry when it has finished cooking. Heat through gently until the lentils are hot, then garnish and serve.

Cajun Chicken Gumbo

This complete main course is cooked in one pan. If you are cooking for one, halve the ingredients—the cooking time should stay the same.

NUTRITIONAL INFORMATION

Calories	425	Sugars	.........8g
Protein	........34g	Fat	..........12g
Carbohydrate	...48g	Saturates	......3g

5 mins   25 mins

SERVES 2

I N G R E D I E N T S

1 tbsp sunflower oil

4 chicken thighs

1 small onion, diced

2 celery stalks, diced

1 small green bell pepper, diced

½ cup long grain rice

1¼ cups chicken bouillon

1 small red chile

8 oz/225 g okra

1 tbsp tomato paste

salt and pepper

1 Heat the oil in a wide pan and fry the chicken until golden. Remove the chicken from the pan.

2 Stir in the diced onion, celery stalks, and bell pepper, and cook for 1 minute. Pour off any excess oil.

3 Add the rice and cook, stirring, for an additional minute. Add the bouillon and heat until boiling. Slice the chile thinly, and trim the okra. Add to the pan with the tomato paste. Season to taste.

4 Return the chicken to the pan and stir. Cover tightly and simmer gently for 15 minutes, or until the rice is tender, the chicken is thoroughly cooked, and the liquid absorbed. Stir occasionally, and if it becomes too dry, add a little extra bouillon.

COOK'S TIP
The whole chile makes the dish hot and spicy—if you prefer a milder flavor, discard the seeds of the chile.

Chicken Tikka

The secret of this very popular dish is that small pieces of chicken are marinated for a minimum of 3 hours in yogurt, garlic, and fragrant spices.

NUTRITIONAL INFORMATION

Calories	327	Sugars	.........2g
Protein	........61g	Fat	...........8g
Carbohydrate	....3g	Saturates	.......1g

15 mins, plus 3 hrs marinating   10 mins

SERVES 6

INGREDIENTS

1 tsp finely chopped fresh root ginger

1 tsp crushed fresh garlic

½ tsp ground coriander

½ tsp ground cumin

1 tsp chili powder

3 tbsp yogurt

1 tsp salt

2 tbsp lemon juice

a few drops of red food coloring (optional)

1 tbsp tomato paste

3 lb 5 oz/1.5 kg chicken breast

1 onion, sliced

3 tbsp oil

TO GARNISH

6 green salad leaves

1 lemon, cut into wedges

3 Using a sharp knife, cut the chicken into bite-size pieces. Add the chicken to the spice mixture and toss to coat well. Leave the to marinate for as long as possible—for a minimum of 3 hours and if possible, overnight.

4 Arrange the onion in the bottom of a heatproof dish. Carefully drizzle half of the oil over the onions.

5 Arrange the marinated chicken pieces on top of the onions and cook under a preheated broiler, turning once and basting with the remaining oil, for approximately 10 minutes, until the chicken is cooked through and tender.

6 Serve on a bed of green salad leaves with warm nans, and garnished with lemon wedges for squeezing.

1 Blend the ginger, garlic, ground coriander, ground cumin, and chili powder thoroughly in a large mixing bowl.

2 Add the yogurt, salt, lemon juice, red food coloring, and tomato paste to the mixing bowl.

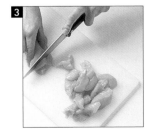

Baked Fish with Basil

Almost any whole fish can be cooked by this method, but snapper, sea bass, and tilapia blend particularly well with the Thai flavors.

NUTRITIONAL INFORMATION

Calories	267	Sugars	.........9g
Protein	........38g	Fat	...........8g
Carbohydrate	....11g	Saturates	.......2g

15 mins   30 mins

SERVES 4

INGREDIENTS

handful of fresh sweet basil leaves

1 lb 10 oz/750 g whole red snapper, sea bass or tilapia, cleaned

2 tbsp groundnut oil

2 tbsp Thai fish sauce

2 garlic cloves, crushed

1 tsp galangal or root ginger, grated finely

2 large red chiles, sliced diagonally

1 yellow pepper, deseeded and diced

1 tbsp palm sugar

1 tbsp rice vinegar

2 tbsp water or fish bouillon

2 tomatoes, deseeded and sliced into thin wedges

1 Reserve a few fresh basil leaves for garnish and tuck the remainder inside the body cavity of the fish.

2 Heat 1 tablespoon of oil in a wide skillet and cook the fish quickly to brown, turning once. Place the fish on a large piece of tinfoil in a roasting pan, and spoon the fish sauce over it. Wrap the tinfoil round the fish loosely, and bake in an oven preheated to 375°F/190°C for 25–30 minutes until just cooked though.

3 Meanwhile, heat the remaining oil and cook the garlic, galangal, and chiles for 30 seconds. Add the pepper and stir-fry for another 2–3 minutes to soften.

4 Stir in the sugar, rice vinegar, and water or bouillon, then add the tomatoes and bring to a boil. Remove the pan from the heat and set aside.

5 Remove the fish from the oven and transfer to a warmed serving plate. Add the fish juices to the pan, then spoon the sauce over the fish and scatter with the reserved basil leaves. Serve immediately.

COOK'S TIP

Large red chiles are less hot than the tiny red bird-eye chiles, so use them freely in cooked dishes such as this for a mild fieriness. Remove the seeds for even milder heat.

Chinese Whole Fried Fish

This impressive dish is ideal for a special dinner, where it will be a talking point. Buy a very fresh, whole fish on the day you plan to cook it.

NUTRITIONAL INFORMATION

Calories 290	Sugars 7g	
Protein 27g	Fat 11g	
Carbohydrate ...23g	Saturates 1g	

🍲 30 mins   🕐 10 mins

SERVES 4–6

INGREDIENTS

6 dried Chinese mushrooms

3 tbsp rice vinegar

2 tbsp brown sugar

3 tbsp dark soy sauce

3 inch/7.5 cm piece fresh root ginger, chopped finely

4 scallions, sliced diagonally

2 tsp cornstarch

2 tbsp lime juice

1 sea bass, about 2 lb 4 oz/1 kg, cleaned

4 tbsp all-purpose flour

sunflower oil for deep frying

salt and pepper

shredded Napa cabbage and radish slices, to serve

1 radish, sliced but left whole, to garnish

1 Soak the dried mushrooms in hot water for about 10 minutes, then drain, reserving a scant ¹/₂ cup of the liquid. Cut the mushrooms into thin slices.

2 Put the reserved mushroom liquid in a pan with the rice vinegar, sugar, soy sauce, and mushrooms, and bring to a boil. Simmer for 3–4 minutes.

3 Add the ginger and scallions, and simmer for 1 minute. Blend the cornstarch and lime juice, stir into the pan and stir for 1–2 minutes until the sauce thickens and clears. Keep to one side while you cook the fish.

4 Season the fish inside and out with salt and pepper, then dust lightly with flour.

5 Heat a 1 inch/2.5 cm depth of oil in a wide, deep pan to 375°F/190°C. Carefully lower the fish into the oil and cook on one side for about 3–4 minutes until golden. Use 2 metal spatulas to turn the fish, then cook on the other side for an additional 3–4 minutes until golden brown.

6 Drain the fish. Serve with shredded Napa cabbage and radish slices, topped with the reheated sauce and garnished with the prepared radish.

Thai-Spiced Salmon

Marinated in delicate Thai spices and quickly pan-fried to perfection, these salmon fillets are a perfect dish for a special dinner.

NUTRITIONAL INFORMATION

Calories	329	Sugars	........0.1g
Protein	........30g	Fat	..........23g
Carbohydrate	...0.1g	Saturates	.......4g

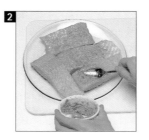

15 mins, plus 30 mins chilling   5 mins

SERVES 4

I N G R E D I E N T S

1 inch/2.5 cm piece grated fresh root ginger

1 tsp coriander seeds, crushed

¼ tsp chili powder

1 tbsp lime juice

1 tsp sesame oil

4 medium salmon fillets with skin

2 tbsp vegetable oil

boiled rice and stir-fried vegetables, to serve

1 Mix the grated root ginger, crushed coriander seeds, and chili powder in a small bowl. Add lime juice and sesame oil.

COOK'S TIP

It is important to use a skillet or a solid griddle for this recipe, so the fish cooks evenly throughout without sticking. If the fish is very thick, turn it carefully to cook on the other side for 2–3 minutes.

2 Place the salmon fillets side by side on a wide, non-metallic plate or dish, and spoon the spice mixture over the flesh side, spreading it to coat each fillet evenly.

3 Cover the dish with plastic wrap and chill the salmon in the refrigerator for 30 minutes for the flavors to penetrate.

4 Pour the oil into a wide, heavy-based skillet or griddle pan and heat it to a high temperature. Place the salmon on the hot pan or griddle, skin side down.

5 Cook the salmon for 4–5 minutes, without turning, until the fillets are crusty underneath and the flesh flakes easily. Transfer immediately to warmed plates and serve at once with the boiled rice and stir-fried vegetables.

Spicy Thai Seafood Stew

This luxurious and deliciously fragrant Thai stew combines mixed seafood with a smooth and spicy coconut sauce.

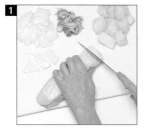

NUTRITIONAL INFORMATION

Calories	288	Sugars	........7g
Protein	........46g	Fat	..........8g
Carbohydrate	...10g	Saturates	.......1g

🗑 20 mins   🕐 5 mins

SERVES 4

I N G R E D I E N T S

7 oz/200 g squid, cleaned

1 lb 2 oz/500 g firm white fish fillet, preferably monkfish or halibut

1 tbsp sunflower oil

4 shallots, chopped finely

2 garlic cloves, chopped finely

2 tbsp green Thai curry paste

2 small lemon grass stems, chopped finely

1 tsp shrimp paste

2¼ cups coconut milk

7 oz/200 g raw jumbo shrimp, peeled and deveined

12 fresh clams in shells, cleaned

8 basil leaves, shredded finely

extra basil leaves, to garnish

boiled rice, to serve

1 Slice the body cavities of the squid into thick rings, using a sharp knife, then cut the firm white fish fillet into bite-size pieces.

2 Heat the oil in a large skillet or a wok and stir-fry the shallots, garlic, and curry paste for 1–2 minutes. Add the lemon grass and shrimp paste, stir in the coconut milk, and bring to a boil. Reduce the heat to simmering point.

3 Add the prepared white fish, squid, and shrimp to the pan, and simmer very gently for 2 minutes.

4 Add the clams to the pan and simmer for another minute until they open. Discard any clams that do not open.

5 Scatter the shredded basil leaves over the stew, and serve immediately with boiled rice, garnished with basil leaves.

COOK'S TIP

Fresh mussels in their shells may be used instead of clams. The white fish may be varied according to taste or availability, but it is best to use fish which stay firm when cooked.

Spicy Scallops with Lime

Really fresh scallops have a delicate flavor and texture, and need only minimal cooking as in this simple stir-fry.

NUTRITIONAL INFORMATION

Calories	145	Sugars 1g
Protein	........17g	Fat 7g
Carbohydrate	....4g	Saturates 3g

10 mins   8 mins

SERVES 4

INGREDIENTS

16 large scallops

1 tbsp butter

1 tbsp vegetable oil

1 tsp garlic, crushed

1 tsp grated fresh root ginger

1 bunch scallions, sliced finely

zest of 1 kaffir lime, grated finely

1 small red chile, deseeded and chopped very finely

3 tbsp kaffir lime juice

salt and pepper

lime wedges and boiled rice, to serve

1 Trim the scallops to remove any black intestine, then wash and pat dry. Separate the corals from the white parts, then slice each white part into 2 rounds.

2 Heat the butter and oil in a skillet or wok. Add the garlic and ginger, and stir-fry for 1 minute without browning. Add the scallions and stir-fry for 1 minute.

3 Add the scallops to the pan and continue stir-frying over a high heat for 4–5 minutes. Stir in the lime zest, chile, and lime juice, and cook for an additional minute. Do not overcook.

4 Serve the scallops hot, with the juices spooned over them, accompanied by lime wedges and boiled rice.

COOK'S TIP

If fresh scallops are not available, frozen ones can be used. Make sure they are thoroughly defrosted before you cook them. Drain off all the excess moisture and pat dry thoroughly with paper towels.

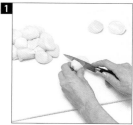  

Shrimp Skewers with Chile

Whole jumbo shrimp cook very quickly on a barbecue grill or under a broiler, so they are ideal for summertime cooking, indoors or outside.

NUTRITIONAL INFORMATION

Calories 106	Sugars 8g	
Protein 11g	Fat 3g	
Carbohydrate 8g	Saturates 1g	

5 mins, plus 2 hrs marinating

6 mins

SERVES 4

INGREDIENTS

1 garlic clove, chopped

1 red bird-eye chile, deseeded and chopped

1 tbsp tamarind paste

1 tbsp sesame oil

1 tbsp dark soy sauce

2 tbsp lime juice

1 tbsp soft light brown sugar

16 large whole raw jumbo shrimp

crusty bread, lime wedges and salad leaves, to serve

1 Put the garlic, chile, tamarind paste, sesame oil, soy sauce, lime juice, and sugar in a small pan. Stir over a low heat until the sugar has completely dissolved, then remove from the heat and let cool.

2 Wash and pat dry the shrimp and place in a single layer in a wide, non-metallic dish. Spoon the marinade over the shrimp and turn them over to coat them evenly. Cover the dish with plastic wrap, and marinate in the refrigerator for at least 2 hours, or preferably overnight.

3 When you are almost ready to cook the shrimp, soak 4 bamboo or wooden skewers in water for about 20 minutes. Drain and dry the skewers, then thread 4 shrimp onto each skewer.

4 Broil the skewered shrimp under a preheated hot broiler for 5–6 minutes, turning them over once, until they turn pink and begin to turn brown. Alternatively, barbecue the skewered shrimp over hot coals.

5 Thread a wedge of lime onto the end of each skewer and serve them with crusty bread and a garnish of salad leaves, arranged attractively.

Thai Green Fish Curry

The pale green curry paste used in this recipe serves as the basis for a range of Thai dishes. It is delicious with chicken and beef, as well as fish.

NUTRITIONAL INFORMATION

Calories	.217	Sugars	.3g
Protein	.12g	Fat	.17g
Carbohydrate	.5g	Saturates	.10g

15 mins   12 mins

SERVES 4

I N G R E D I E N T S

2 tbsp vegetable oil

1 garlic clove, chopped

1 small eggplant, diced

½ cup coconut cream

2 tbsp Thai fish sauce

1 tsp sugar

8 oz/225 g firm white fish such as cod, haddock, halibut, cut into pieces

½ cup fish bouillon

2 lime leaves, shredded finely

about 15 leaves Thai basil, if available, or ordinary basil

plain boiled rice or noodles, to serve

G R E E N   C U R R Y   P A S T E

5 green chiles, deseeded and chopped

2 tsp chopped lemon grass

1 large shallot, chopped

2 garlic cloves, chopped

1 tsp freshly grated ginger or galangal

2 coriander roots, chopped

½ tsp ground coriander

¼ tsp ground cumin

1 kaffir lime leaf, chopped finely

1 tsp shrimp paste (optional)

½ tsp salt

1 To make the curry paste, put all the ingredients into a blender or a spice grinder and blend to a smooth paste, adding a little water if necessary.

2 In a skillet or a wok, heat the oil until it is almost smoking and cook the garlic until golden. Stir-fry the curry paste for a few seconds, then add the eggplant. Stir-fry for 4–5 minutes until softened.

3 Add the coconut cream. Bring to a boil and stir until the cream thickens. Add the fish sauce and sugar and stir into the mixture.

4 Add the fish and bouillon. Simmer for 3–4 minutes, stirring occasionally, until the fish is just tender. Add the lime leaves and basil, and then cook for another minute. Serve with noodles.

Mackerel Escabeche

Although *escabeche*—meaning pickled in vinegar—is a Spanish word, variations of this dish are to be found all over the Mediterranean region.

NUTRITIONAL INFORMATION

Calories	750	Sugars	.........3g
Protein	........33g	Fat	..........63g
Carbohydrate	...12g	Saturates	......11g

10 mins, plus 8 hrs cooling　　10 mins

SERVES 4

INGREDIENTS

⅔ cup olive oil

4 mackerel, filleted

2 tbsp all-purpose flour, seasoned with salt and pepper, for dusting

4 tbsp red wine vinegar

1 onion, sliced finely

1 strip orange rind, removed with a potato peeler

1 sprig fresh thyme

1 sprig fresh rosemary

1 fresh bay leaf

4 garlic cloves, crushed

2 fresh red chiles, bruised

1 tsp salt

3 tbsp chopped fresh flat-leaf parsley

crusty bread, to serve

1 Heat half the oil in a skillet and dust the mackerel fillets with the seasoned flour. Shake off any excess flour.

2 Add the fish to the skillet and cook for about 30 seconds on each side. (The mackerel will not be cooked through at this point.)

3 Transfer the mackerel to a shallow dish, large enough to hold all the fillets in a single layer.

4 Add the the vinegar, onion, orange zest, thyme, rosemary, bay leaf, garlic, chiles, and salt to the pan. Simmer together for 10 minutes.

5 Add the remaining olive oil and the chopped parsley to the pan and stir to combine with the other ingredients. Pour the mixture over the fish and leave until it has cooled, or, preferably, overnight. Serve cold with plenty of crusty bread.

VARIATION
Substitute 12 whole sardines, cleaned, with heads removed. Cook in the same way. Tuna steaks are also delicious served escabeche.

Red Shrimp Curry

Like all Thai curries, this one has as its base a hot paste of chili and spices and a delicious sauce of coconut milk.

NUTRITIONAL INFORMATION

Calories	149	Sugars 4g
Protein	........15g	Fat 7g
Carbohydrate	....6g	Saturates 1g

10 mins · 10 mins

SERVES 4

INGREDIENTS

2 tbsp vegetable oil

1 garlic clove, chopped finely

1 tbsp red curry paste

scant 1 cup coconut milk

2 tbsp Thai fish sauce

1 tsp sugar

12 large raw shrimp, deveined

2 lime leaves, shredded finely

1 small red chile, deseeded and sliced
 finely

10 leaves Thai basil, if available,
 or ordinary basil

RED CURRY PASTE

3 dried long red chilis

½ tsp ground coriander

¼ tsp ground cumin

½ tsp ground black pepper

2 garlic cloves, chopped

2 stems lemon grass, chopped

1 kaffir lime leaf, chopped finely

1 tsp freshly grated root ginger or
 galangal, if available

1 tsp shrimp paste (optional)

½ tsp salt

1 To make the red curry paste, put all the ingredients in a blender or a spice grinder and blend to a smooth paste, adding a little water if necessary. Alternatively, pound the ingredients using a mortar and pestle until smooth.

2 Heat the oil in a wok or a skillet until almost smoking. Add the garlic and cook until golden. Add 1 tablespoon of the curry paste and cook for 1 minute. Add half the coconut milk, the fish sauce, and the sugar. The mixture will thicken slightly.

3 Add the shrimp and simmer for 3–4 minutes until they turn color. Add the remaining coconut milk, the lime leaves, and the chile. Cook for 2–3 minutes until the shrimp are just tender.

4 Add the basil leaves, stir until wilted, and serve immediately.

Curried Shrimp with Zucchini

This curry will be very quick to cook if you prepare everything carefully beforehand—including measuring out the spices.

NUTRITIONAL INFORMATION

Calories 272	Sugars 5g
Protein 29g	Fat 15g
Carbohydrate 5g	Saturates 2g

 10 mins, plus 30 mins standing   10 mins

SERVES 4

I N G R E D I E N T S

12 oz/350 g small zucchini

1 tsp salt

1 lb/450 g cooked jumbo shrimp

5 tbsp vegetable oil

4 garlic cloves, chopped finely

5 tbsp chopped cilantro

1 fresh green chile, deseeded and chopped finely

½ tsp ground turmeric

1½ tsp ground cumin

pinch cayenne pepper

7 oz/200 g canned chopped tomatoes

1 tsp freshly grated ginger

1 tbsp lemon juice

steamed basmati rice, to serve

1 Cut the zucchini into small batons. Put into a colander and sprinkle with a little of the salt. Set aside for 30 minutes. Rinse, drain, and pat dry. Spread the shrimp on paper towels to drain.

2 In a wok or a skillet, heat the oil over a high heat. Add the garlic. As soon as the garlic begins to brown, add the zucchini, cilantro, green chile, turmeric, cumin, cayenne, tomatoes and their juices, ginger, lemon juice, and remaining salt. Stir well and bring to a boil.

3 Cover and simmer over a low heat for about 5 minutes. Uncover the pan and add the shrimp.

4 Increase the heat and simmer for 5 minutes to reduce the liquid to a thick sauce. Serve immediately with steamed basmati rice, garnished with lime wedges.

VARIATION
If you can't find cooked jumbo shrimp for this recipe, use cooked peeled shrimp instead, but these release quite a lot of liquid so you may need to increase the final simmering time to thicken the sauce.

Coconut Rice with Monkfish

This Thai-influenced rice dish, cooked in coconut milk and tomatoes, and topped with spicy marinated monkfish, makes an unusual one-pot meal.

NUTRITIONAL INFORMATION

Calories 440	Sugars 8g	
Protein 22g	Fat 14g	
Carbohydrate . . .60g	Saturates 2g	

10 mins, plus 20 mins marinating

30 mins

SERVES 4

I N G R E D I E N T S

1 hot red chile, deseeded and chopped

1 tsp crushed chili flakes

2 garlic cloves, chopped

2 pinches saffron

3 tbsp roughly chopped mint leaves

4 tbsp olive oil

2 tbsp lemon juice

12 oz/375 g monkfish fillet, cut into bite-size pieces

1 onion, chopped finely

8 oz/225 g long grain rice

14 oz/400g canned chopped tomatoes

¾ cup coconut milk

1 cup frozen peas

salt and pepper

2 tbsp chopped cilantro, to garnish

1 In a food processor or a blender, process the chile and the crushed chili flakes, garlic, saffron, mint, olive oil, and lemon juice, until the ingredients are chopped finely but the mixture is not smooth.

2 Put the monkfish pieces into a non-metallic dish and pour the spice paste over them, mixing together well. Set aside for 20 minutes to marinate.

3 Heat a large pan until it very hot. Using a slotted spoon, lift the monkfish pieces from the marinade and add them in batches to the hot pan. Cook for 3–4 minutes until browned and firm. Remove the fish pieces with a slotted spoon and set them aside.

4 Add the onion and remaining marinade to the same pan and cook for 5 minutes until softened and lightly browned. Add the rice and stir until well coated. Add the tomatoes and coconut milk. Bring to a boil, cover, and simmer very gently for 15 minutes. Stir in the peas, season, and arrange the fish over the top. Cover with tinfoil and continue to cook over a very low heat for 5 minutes. Serve garnished with the chopped cilantro.

Spicy Broiled Salmon

The woody smoked flavors of the chipotle chile are mixed with spices and zesty lime and used to marinate salmon for broiling.

NUTRITIONAL INFORMATION

Calories 419	Sugars 2g
Protein 41g	Fat 28g
Carbohydrate 2g	Saturates 5g

🍧 🍧

🧊 10 mins, plus
1 hr marinating   🕐 8 mins

SERVES 4

I N G R E D I E N T S

4 medium salmon steaks

lime slices, to garnish

MARINADE

4 garlic cloves

2 tbsp extra-virgin olive oil

pinch of ground allspice

pinch of ground cinnamon

juice of 2 limes

1–2 tsp marinade from canned chipotle chilis or bottled chipotle chili salsa

¼ tsp ground cumin

pinch of sugar

salt and pepper

TO SERVE

tomato wedges

3 scallions, chopped finely

shredded lettuce

1 To make the marinade, chop the garlic finely and place in a bowl with the olive oil, allspice, cinnamon, lime juice, chipotle marinade, cumin, and sugar. Add salt and pepper, and stir to combine.

2 Coat the salmon with the garlic mixture, then place in a non-metallic dish. Leave it to marinate for at least an hour or overnight in the refrigerator.

3 Transfer to a broiler pan and cook under a preheated broiler for 3–4 minutes on each side. Alternatively, cook the salmon over hot coals on a barbecue grill.

4 To serve, mix the tomato wedges with the scallions. Place the salmon on individual plates and arrange the tomato salad and shredded lettuce alongside. Garnish with lime slices and serve immediately.

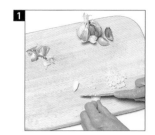

VARIATION
The marinade also goes well with fresh tuna steaks.

Mackerel with Lime

The secret of this barbecue grilled dish lies in the fresh flavors of lime and coriander which perfectly complement oily fish such as mackerel.

NUTRITIONAL INFORMATION

Calories 302	Sugars 0g
Protein 21g	Fat 24g
Carbohydrate 0g	Saturates 4g

 10 mins   10 mins

SERVES 4

INGREDIENTS

4 small mackerel

¼ tsp ground coriander

¼ tsp ground cumin

4 sprigs cilantro

3 tbsp chopped cilantro

1 red chile, deseeded and chopped

grated zest and juice of 1 lime

2 tbsp sunflower oil

salt and pepper

1 lime, sliced, to garnish

chile flowers (optional), to garnish

mixed salad greens, to serve

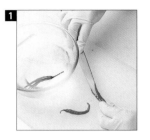
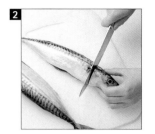

1 To make the chile flowers (if using), cut the tip of a small chile lengthwise into thin strips, leaving the chile intact at the stem end. Remove the seeds and place the chile strips in iced water until curled.

COOK'S TIP

This recipe is suitable for other oily fish, such as trout, herring, or sardines. You can ask the fish dealer to gut the fish for you.

2 If the mackerel are intact, clean and gut them, removing the heads if you prefer the fish without them. Transfer the cleaned mackerel to a chopping board.

3 Sprinkle the fish inside and outside with the ground coriander and cumin and salt and pepper to taste. The sprinkle 1 teaspoon of the chopped fresh cilantro evenly inside the cavity of each of the gutted mackerel.

4 Mix together the remaining cilantro, chile, grated lime zest and lime juice, and the sunflower oil in a small bowl. Brush liberally over both sides of the fish.

5 Place the fish in a hinged rack and grill over hot coals for 3–4 minutes on each side, turning once. Brush often with the basting mixture. Transfer to plates and garnish with chile flowers (if using) and lime slices. Serve with mixed salad greens.

Szechuan White Fish

Hot Szechuan pepper is not related to the black pepper in common use, but is the dried berry of a shrub of the citrus family.

NUTRITIONAL INFORMATION

Calories	225	Sugars	.........3g
Protein	........20g	Fat	...........8g
Carbohydrate	...17g	Saturates	.......1g

🍠 10 mins 🕐 15 mins

SERVES 4

INGREDIENTS

12 oz/350 g white fish fillets

1 small egg, beaten

3 tbsp all-purpose flour

4 tbsp dry white wine

3 tbsp light soy sauce

vegetable oil, for deep frying

1 garlic clove, cut into slivers

½ inch/1 cm piece fresh root ginger, chopped finely

1 onion, chopped finely

1 celery stalk, chopped

1 fresh red chile, chopped

3 scallions, chopped

1 tsp rice wine vinegar

½ tsp ground Szechuan pepper

¾ cup fish bouillon

1 tsp superfine sugar

1 tsp cornstarch

2 tsp water

1 Cut the fish into 1½ inch/4 cm cubes. Beat together the egg, flour, wine, and 1 tablespoon of soy sauce to make a batter. Dip the cubes of fish into the batter to coat well.

2 Heat the oil in a wok, reduce the heat slightly, and cook the fish in batches, for 2–3 minutes, until golden brown. Remove with a slotted spoon, drain on paper towels, set aside, and keep warm.

3 Cool the oil, then pour all but approximately 1 tablespoon from the wok and return to the heat. Add the garlic, ginger, onion, celery, chile, and scallions, and stir-fry for 1–2 minutes. Stir in the remaining soy sauce and the vinegar.

4 Add the Szechuan pepper, bouillon, and sugar to the wok. Mix the cornstarch with the water to form a smooth paste and stir it into the bouillon. Bring to a boil and cook, stirring, for 1 minute, until the sauce thickens and clears.

5 Return the fish cubes to the wok and cook the fish for 1–2 minutes. Serve them immediately, while very hot.

Indonesian-Style Spicy Cod

A delicious aromatic coating of coconut and spices makes this dish rather special. Serve it with a crisp salad and crusty bread.

NUTRITIONAL INFORMATION

Calories	146	Sugars	.........2g
Protein	........19g	Fat	..........7g
Carbohydrate	....2g	Saturates	......4g

10 mins   15 mins

SERVES 4

I N G R E D I E N T S

4 medium cod steaks

1 stem lemon grass

1 small red onion, chopped

3 cloves garlic, chopped

2 fresh red chiles, deseeded and chopped

1 tsp grated fresh root ginger

¼ tsp turmeric

2 tbsp butter, cut into small cubes

8 tbsp coconut milk

2 tbsp lemon juice

salt and pepper

red chiles, to garnish (optional)

1 Rinse the cod steaks and pat them dry on absorbent paper towels.

2 Remove and discard the outer leaves from the lemon grass, and slice the inner section thinly.

3 Place the lemon grass, onion, garlic, chiles, ginger, and turmeric in a food processor and blend until the ingredients are all just chopped finely. Season with salt and pepper to taste.

4 With the processor running, add the butter, coconut milk, and lemon juice, and process until well blended.

5 Place the fish in a shallow, non-metallic dish. Pour the coconut mixture over it, and turn the fish to coat it evenly on both sides.

6 Place the fish steaks in a hinged basket, if you have one, or on a grill and cook over hot coals for 15 minutes or until the fish is cooked through, turning once. Serve garnished with red chiles (if using).

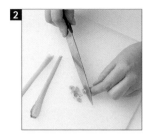

COOK'S TIP

If you prefer a milder flavor, omit the chiles altogether. For a hotter flavor do not remove the seeds from one or both the chiles.

Hot & Sour Beef Salad

The Thais are primarily fish-eaters, so beef appears on the menu mainly on feast days. This dish demonstrates that a little beef can go a long way.

NUTRITIONAL INFORMATION

Calories 207   Sugars 7g
Protein . . . . .15g   Fat 13g
Carbohydrate . . . .9g   Saturates 3g

 15 mins   4 mins

SERVES 4

I N G R E D I E N T S

1 tsp black peppercorns
1 tsp coriander seeds
1 dried red bird-eye chile
¼ tsp five-spice powder
9 oz/250 g beef tenderloin
1 tbsp dark soy sauce
6 scallions
1 carrot
¼ cucumber
8 radishes
1 red onion
¼ head bok choy
2 tbsp groundnut oil
1 garlic clove, crushed
1 tsp finely chopped lemon grass
1 tbsp chopped fresh mint
1 tbsp chopped cilantro

D R E S S I N G

3 tbsp lime juice
1 tbsp light soy sauce
2 tsp brown sugar
1 tsp sesame oil

1 Crush the peppercorns, coriander seeds, and chile with a pestle and mortar, then mix with the five-spice powder and sprinkle on a plate. Brush the beef all over with soy sauce, then roll it in the spices to coat evenly.

2 Cut the scallions into 2½ inch/6 cm lengths and then shred them finely lengthwise. Place in iced water and leave until curled. Drain well.

3 Trim the carrot and cut into very thin diagonal slices. Halve the cucumber and scoop out the seeds, then slice thinly. Trim the radishes and cut into flower shapes.

4 Cut the onion into vertical slices. Shred the bok choy. Toss the vegetables together in a large salad bowl.

5 Heat the oil in a heavy-based skillet and cook the garlic and lemon grass until they just turn golden brown. Add the steak and press down with a spatula to brown it evenly. Cook for 3–4 minutes, turning it over once. Remove the pan from the heat.

6 Slice the steak thinly and toss it into the salad with the mint and cilantro. Mix the ingredients for the dressing, stir the mixture into the pan, then spoon it over the salad.

Papaya & Avocado Salad

This colorful and refreshing salad, with its sweet and spicy flavors, is the perfect foil for a meaty main dish and makes a light summer lunch.

NUTRITIONAL INFORMATION

Calories 194	Sugars 7g	
Protein 4g	Fat 16g	
Carbohydrate 9g	Saturates 3g	

🍴 10 mins   🕐 0 mins

SERVES 4–6

INGREDIENTS

7 oz/200 g mixed salad greens

2–3 scallions, chopped

3–4 tbsp chopped cilantro

1 small papaya

2 red bell peppers

1 avocado

1 tbsp lime juice

3–4 tbsp pumpkin seeds, toasted (optional)

DRESSING

juice of 1 lime

large pinch of paprika

large pinch of ground cumin

large pinch of sugar

1 garlic clove, chopped finely

4 tbsp extra-virgin olive oil

dash of white wine vinegar (optional)

salt

1 Combine the salad greens with the scallions and cilantro. Mix well, then transfer the salad to a large serving dish.

2 Cut the papaya in half and scoop out the seeds with a spoon. Cut the fruit into quarters, remove the peel, and slice the flesh. Arrange the slices on top of the salad greens. Cut the bell peppers in half,

remove the cores and seeds, then slice the flesh thinly and add the sliced peppers to the salad greens.

3 Cut the avocado in half around the pit. Twist apart, then remove the pit with a knife. Carefully peel off the skin, dice the flesh. and toss in lime juice to prevent the avocado from discoloring. Add to the other salad ingredients.

4 To make the salad dressing, whisk together the lime juice, paprika, ground cumin, sugar, garlic, and olive oil. Taste and add salt as required.

5 Pour the dressing over the salad and toss lightly, adding a dash of wine vinegar if you prefer a more intense flavor. For still more flavor, sprinkle with the toasted pumpkin seeds.

Mexican Potato Salad

This dish is full of enticing Mexican flavors. Potato slices are topped with tomatoes, chile, and bell peppers, and served with a guacamole dressing.

NUTRITIONAL INFORMATION

Calories	260	Sugars	.........6g
Protein	.........6g	Fat	...........9g
Carbohydrate	...41g	Saturates	......2g

 10 mins, plus 30 mins cooling   15 mins

SERVES 4

I N G R E D I E N T S

4 large waxy potatoes, sliced

1 ripe avocado

1 tsp olive oil

1 tsp lemon juice

1 garlic clove, crushed

1 onion, chopped

2 large tomatoes, sliced

1 green chile, chopped

1 yellow bell pepper, sliced

2 tbsp chopped cilantro

salt and pepper

lemon wedges, to garnish

1 Cook the potato slices in a pan of boiling water for 10-15 minutes or until tender. Drain and leave to cool.

2 Meanwhile, cut the avocado in half and remove the pit. Using a spoon, scoop the avocado flesh from the 2 halves and place in a mixing bowl.

3 Mash the avocado flesh with a fork and stir in the olive oil, lemon juice, garlic, and chopped onion. Cover the bowl and set aside.

4 Mix the tomatoes, chile, and yellow bell pepper, and transfer them to a salad bowl with the potato slices.

5 Spoon the avocado mixture on top of the salad base and sprinkle with the cilantro. Season to taste and serve garnished with lemon wedges.

COOK'S TIP
Choose a ripe avocado that yields to gentle pressure from your thumb. Mixing the avocado flesh with lemon juice prevents it from turning brown once exposed to the air.

Potato & Chicken Salad

The spicy peanut dressing served with this salad may be prepared in advance and left to chill a day before required.

NUTRITIONAL INFORMATION

Calories	802	Sugars	........15g
Protein	........35g	Fat	..........55g
Carbohydrate	...45g	Saturates	......10g

 5 mins   15 mins

SERVES 4

INGREDIENTS

4 large waxy potatoes

10½ oz/300 g fresh pineapple, diced

2 carrots, grated

6 oz/175 g bean sprouts

1 bunch scallions, sliced

1 large zucchini, cut into short thin sticks

3 celery stalks, cut into short thin sticks

generous 1 cup unsalted peanuts

2 medium cooked chicken breast fillets, sliced

DRESSING

6 tbsp crunchy peanut butter

6 tbsp olive oil

2 tbsp light soy sauce

1 red chile, chopped

2 tsp sesame oil

4 tsp lime juice

1 Cut the potatoes into small dice and cook in a pan of boiling water for 10 minutes or until tender. Drain and leave to cool, then transfer to a salad bowl.

2 Add the pineapple, carrots, bean sprouts, scallions, zucchini, celery, peanuts, and sliced chicken to the potatoes. Toss the ingredients well.

3 To make the dressing, put the peanut butter in a small mixing bowl and gradually whisk in the olive oil and light soy sauce. Stir in the chopped red chile, sesame oil, and lime juice. Mix until well combined.

4 Pour the spicy dressing over the salad and toss lightly to coat all of the ingredients. Serve immediately.

COOK'S TIP

Unsweetened canned pineapple may be used in place of the fresh pineapple for convenience. If only sweetened canned pineapple is available, drain it, and rinse under cold running water before using.

Gingered Potatoes

This is a simple spicy dish which is ideal with a plain main course.
The cashew nuts and celery add extra crunch.

NUTRITIONAL INFORMATION

Calories 325	Sugars 1g
Protein 5g	Fat 21g
Carbohydrate ...30g	Saturates 9g

10 mins  25 mins

SERVES 4

INGREDIENTS

1½ lb/675 g waxy potatoes, cubed

few strands of saffron

2 tbsp vegetable oil

2 inch/5 cm piece of root ginger, grated

1 green chile, chopped

1 celery stalk, chopped

¼ cup cashew nuts

3 tbsp boiling water

¼ cup butter

celery leaves, to garnish

1 Cook the potatoes in a pan of boiling water for 10 minutes, then drain thoroughly.

2 Place the saffron strands in a small bowl. Add the boiling water and set the bowl aside. Leave the saffron to soak for approximately 5 minutes.

3 Heat the oil in a heavy-based skillet and add the potatoes. Cook over a medium heat, stirring constantly, for 3-4 minutes.

4 Add the grated ginger, chile, celery, and cashew nuts, and cook for 1 minute.

5 Add the butter to the pan, lower the heat, and stir in the saffron mixture. Cook over a low heat for 10 minutes, or until the potatoes are tender.

6 Transfer to a warm serving dish, garnish the gingered potatoes with the celery leaves, and serve at once.

COOK'S TIP

Use a non-stick, heavy-based skillet because the potato mixture is fairly dry and may tend to stick to a pan with a metal surface.

Stir-Fried Ginger Mushrooms

This quick vegetarian stir-fry is rather like a rich curry. It is full of warm spices and garlic, whose flavors are balanced with creamy coconut milk.

NUTRITIONAL INFORMATION

Calories	174	Sugars	.........7g
Protein	.........8g	Fat	...........9g
Carbohydrate	...15g	Saturates	.......1g

 10 mins   10 mins

SERVES 4

INGREDIENTS

2 tbsp vegetable oil

3 garlic cloves, crushed

1 tbsp Thai red curry paste

½ tsp turmeric

14½ oz/425 g canned Chinese straw mushrooms, drained and halved

¾ inch/2 cm piece fresh root ginger, shredded finely

scant ½ cup coconut milk

1 cup dried Chinese black mushrooms, soaked, drained, and sliced

1 tbsp lemon juice

1 tbsp light soy sauce

2 tsp sugar

½ tsp salt

8 cherry tomatoes, halved

7oz/200 g firm tofu, diced

cilantro leaves, to garnish

boiled fragrant rice, to serve

COOK'S TIP

You can vary the mushrooms depending on your own taste. Try a mixture of oyster and shiitake for a change—or try cultivated white mushrooms.

1 Heat the oil and cook the garlic for approximately 1 minute, stirring constantly. Stir in the curry paste and turmeric, and cook for another 30 seconds.

2 Add in the straw mushrooms and ginger, and stir-fry for 2 minutes. Mix in the coconut milk and bring to a boil. Add the dried Chinese black mushrooms, lemon juice, soy sauce, sugar, and salt, stir well, and heat thoroughly.

3 Add the tomatoes and tofu and toss gently to heat through.

4 Scatter the cilantro over the mixture and serve hot, with rice.

Roasted Thai-Spiced Peppers

This is a colorful side dish that also makes a good buffet party salad. It is best made in advance to give time for the flavors to mingle.

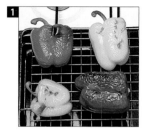

NUTRITIONAL INFORMATION

Calories 83	Sugars 17g
Protein 2g	Fat 1g
Carbohydrate ...17g	Saturates 0.1g

 5 mins, plus 1 hr chilling   15 mins

SERVES 4

INGREDIENTS

2 red bell peppers

2 yellow bell peppers

2 green bell peppers

2 red bird-eye chiles, deseeded and chopped finely

1 lemon grass stem, shredded finely

4 tbsp lime juice

2 tbsp palm sugar

1 tbsp Thai fish sauce

1 Roast the bell peppers under a hot broiler, or in a hot oven, turning them over occasionally until the skins are charred. Cool slightly, then remove the skins. Cut each in half and remove the core and seeds.

2 Slice the peppers thickly and transfer to a large mixing bowl.

3 Put the chiles, lemon grass, lime juice, sugar, and Thai fish sauce into a screw-top jar and shake it well until they are thoroughly mixed.

4 Pour the dressing evenly over the peppers. Allow to cool completely, cover with plastic wrap, and chill in the refrigerator for at least an hour before transferring to a serving dish.

COOK'S TIP

The flavors will mingle best if the peppers are still slightly warm when you spoon the dressing over them. Prepare the dressing while the peppers are cooking, ready to pour over them when cooked.

Zucchini & Tomato Salad

Lightly cooked zucchini are mixed with ripe, juicy tomatoes and dressed with a chile vinaigrette to create a perfect side salad.

NUTRITIONAL INFORMATION

Calories 92	Sugars 3g	
Protein 2g	Fat 8g	
Carbohydrate 4g	Saturates 1g	

10 mins, plus 20 mins standing

20 mins

SERVES 4–6

INGREDIENTS

1 large mild green chile, or a combination of 1 green bell pepper and ½–1 green chile

4 zucchini, sliced

2–3 garlic cloves, chopped finely

pinch sugar

¼ tsp ground cumin

2 tbsp white wine vinegar

4 tbsp extra-virgin olive oil

2–3 tbsp cilantro

4 ripe tomatoes, diced or sliced

salt and pepper

1 Roast the mild chile, or the combination of the green bell pepper and chile, in a heavy-based ungreased skillet or under a preheated broiler until the skin is charred. Place in a plastic bag, twist to seal well and leave the charred vegetables to stand for 20 minutes.

2 Peel the skin from the chile and bell pepper, if using, then carefully remove the seeds and slice the flesh fairly thinly. Keep to one side.

3 Bring about 2 inches/5 cm water to a boil in the bottom of a steamer. Add the zucchini to the top part of the steamer, cover, and steam for about 5 minutes until just tender.

4 Meanwhile, combine the garlic, sugar, cumin, vinegar, olive oil, and cilantro thoroughly in a bowl. Stir in the chile and bell pepper, if using, then season with salt and pepper to taste.

5 Arrange the zucchini and tomatoes in a serving bowl or on a platter and spoon over the chile dressing. Serve the salad immediately.

VARIATION

Add 8oz/225 g cooked peeled shrimp to the salad before coating with the dressing in Step 5.

Spicy Cauliflower

This is a perfectly delicious way to serve cauliflower. It can be enjoyed as a salad or at a picnic, or as a side dish to a main meal.

NUTRITIONAL INFORMATION

Calories ....68 Sugars 3g
Protein ....5g Fat 4g
Carbohydrate ....4g Saturates 1g

 5 mins   15 mins

SERVES 4

INGREDIENTS

1 lb 2 oz/500 g cauliflower, cut into florets

1 tbsp sunflower oil

1 garlic clove

½ tsp turmeric

1 tsp cumin seeds, ground

1 tsp coriander seeds, ground

1 tsp yellow mustard seeds

12 scallions, sliced finely

salt and pepper

1 Cook the cauliflower lightly in boiling water, drain, and set aside.

2 Heat the oil gently in a large, heavy-based skillet or a wok. Add the whole garlic clove, turmeric, ground cumin, ground coriander, and mustard seeds. Stir well and cover the pan.

3 When the mustard seeds start to pop, add the scallions and stir. Cook for 2 minutes, stirring constantly, to soften them a little. Season to taste.

4 Add the cauliflower and stir for 3–4 minutes until coated completely with the spices and heated through.

5 Remove the garlic clove from the pan and serve immediately.

COOK'S TIP

For a special occasion this dish looks great made with baby cauliflowers instead of florets. Peel off most of the outer leaves, leaving a few for decoration, blanch the cauliflowers whole for 4 minutes, and drain. Continue as in step 2.

Exotic Fruit Salad

This colorful fruit salad, infused with the delicate flavors of jasmine tea and ginger, makes an exotic, light dessert.

NUTRITIONAL INFORMATION

Calories 65   Sugars 16g
Protein ....1g   Fat 0g
Carbohydrate ...16g   Saturates 0g

15 mins, plus 1 hr chilling   0 mins

SERVES 6

INGREDIENTS

1 tsp jasmine tea

1 tsp grated fresh root ginger

1 strip lime zest

½ cup boiling water

2 tbsp superfine sugar

1 paw-paw

1 mango

½ small pineapple

1 starfruit

2 passion fruit

juice of ½–1 lime

1 Place the tea, root ginger, and lime zest in a heatproof pitcher, and pour over the boiling water. Leave to infuse for 5 minutes, then strain the liquid.

2 Add the sugar to the liquid and stir well to dissolve. Leave the syrup until it is completely cool.

3 Halve, deseed, and peel the paw-paw. Halve the mango, remove the pit and peel. Peel and remove the core from the pineapple. Cut all the prepared fruits into bite-sized pieces.

4 Slice the starfruit crossways. Place all the prepared fruits in a wide serving bowl and pour the cooled syrup over them. Cover the bowl with plastic wrap and chill the mixture for about 1 hour.

5 Cut the passion fruit in half, scoop out the flesh, and mix with the lime juice. Spoon over the salad and serve.

COOK'S TIP

Starfruit have little flavor when unripe and green, but once ripened and turned yellow they become delicately sweet and fragrant. Usually by this stage, the tips of the ridges have become brown, so you will need to remove these before slicing.

Lychee & Ginger Sorbet

A refreshing last course after a rich meal, this quick and simple sorbet can be served alone or with fruit salad.

NUTRITIONAL INFORMATION

Calories 159	Sugars 40g	
Protein 2g	Fat 0g	
Carbohydrate ...40g	Saturates 0g	

5 mins, plus 5–6 hrs freezing   0 mins

SERVES 4

INGREDIENTS

28 oz/800 g canned lychees in syrup

zest of 1 lime, grated finely

2 tbsp lime juice

3 tbsp candied ginger syrup

2 egg whites

TO DECORATE

starfruit slices

slivers of candied ginger

1 Drain the lychees, reserving the syrup. Place the fruits in a blender or a food processor with the lime rind, juice, and candied ginger syrup, and process until completely smooth. Transfer to a mixing bowl.

2 Mix the purée thoroughly with the reserved lychee syrup, then pour into a freezerproof container and freeze for 1–1½ hours until slushy in texture. (Alternatively, use an ice-cream maker.)

3 Remove from the freezer and whisk to break up the ice crystals. Whisk the egg whites in a clean, dry bowl with a whisk until they rise in stiff peaks, then fold quickly and lightly into the iced mixture.

4 Return the mixture to the freezer and freeze until firm. Remove the sorbet from the freezer to the refrigerator 20 minutes before needed. Serve in scoops, and decorate with slices of starfruit and ginger.

COOK'S TIP

It is not recommended that raw egg whites are served to very young children, pregnant women, the elderly or anyone weakened by chronic illness.

Steamed Coconut Cake

This steamed coconut cake, steeped in a lime and ginger syrup, is very typical of Thai desserts and sweets, and has a distinctly Chinese influence.

NUTRITIONAL INFORMATION

Calories 243	Sugars 17g	
Protein 4g	Fat 12g	
Carbohydrate ...31g	Saturates 8g	

 15 mins   30 mins

SERVES 8

INGREDIENTS

2 extra large eggs, separated

pinch of salt

½ cup superfine sugar

5 tbsp butter, melted and cooled

5 tbsp coconut milk

1¼ cups self-rising flour

½ tsp baking powder

3 tbsp shredded coconut

4 tbsp candied ginger syrup

3 tbsp lime juice

TO DECORATE

3 pieces candied ginger, diced

curls of fresh grated coconut

strips of lime zest

1 Cut an 11 inch/28 cm round of non-stick parchment and press into a 7 inch/18 cm steamer basket to line it.

COOK'S TIP

Coconuts grow on tropical beaches all around the world, but probably originated in South East Asia, and it is here that coconut is most important in cooking.

2 Whisk the egg whites with the salt until stiff. Gradually whisk in the sugar, 1 tablespoon at a time, whisking hard after each addition until the mixture stands in stiff peaks.

3 Whisk in the yolks, then quickly stir in the butter and coconut milk. Sift the flour and baking powder over the mixture, then fold in lightly and evenly with a large metal spoon. Fold in the coconut.

4 Spoon the mixture into the lined steamer basket and tuck the spare paper over the top. Place the basket over boiling water, cover, and steam for 30 minutes.

5 Turn the cake onto a plate, remove the paper, and cool slightly. Mix the ginger syrup and lime juice, and spoon the mixture over the cake. Cut into squares and top with ginger, coconut, and lime zest.

Melon & Ginger Crush

A really refreshing summer drink, this melon crush is quick and simple to make. Use ordinary limes if you cannot find kaffir limes.

NUTRITIONAL INFORMATION

Calories	46	Sugars	.........7g
Protein	.........1g	Fat	...........0g
Carbohydrate	....7g	Saturates	.......0g

 5 mins   0 mins

SERVES 4

I N G R E D I E N T S

1 melon, about 1 lb 12 oz/800 g

6 tbsp ginger wine

3 tbsp kaffir lime juice

ice, crushed

1 lime

1 Peel and deseed the melon and roughly chop the flesh. Place it in a blender or food processor with the ginger wine and the lime juice.

2 Blend on high speed until the mixture is completely smooth.

3 Put plenty of crushed ice into 4 tall tumblers. Pour the melon and ginger crush over the ice.

4 Cut the lime into slim slices, cut a slit in each one and slip it onto the side of a glass. Serve immediately.

VARIATION

For a non-alcoholic version of this drink, omit the ginger wine, then top up the glass with ginger ale. For a seasonal change of flavor, use a watermelon.

This is a Parragon Publishing Book
This edition published in 2003

Parragon Publishing
Queen Street House
4 Queen Street
Bath BA1 1HE, UK

ISBN: 1-40540-876-6

Printed in China

NOTE

This book uses metric and imperial measurements. Follow the same units
of measurement throughout; do not mix metric and imperial.
All spoon measurements are level: teaspoons are assumed to be 5 ml, and
tablespoons are assumed to be 15 ml. Unless otherwise stated,
milk is assumed to be full fat, eggs and individual vegetables such as potatoes
are medium, and pepper is freshly ground black pepper.

The nutritional information provided for each recipe is per serving or per person.
Optional ingredients, variations or serving suggestions have
not been included in the calculations. The times given for each recipe are an approximate
guide only because the preparation times may differ according to the techniques used by
different people and the cooking times may vary as a result of the type of oven used.

Recipes using raw or very lightly cooked eggs should be
avoided by infants, the elderly, pregnant women, convalescents,
and anyone suffering from an illness.

The publisher would like to thank
Steamer Trading Cookshop, Lewes, East Sussex, for the kind loan of props.